FEVER DREAM: SOUTHSIDE

Douglas Maxwell

FEVER DREAM: SOUTHSIDE

OBERON BOOKS
LONDON

WWW.OBERONBOOKS.COM

First published in 2015 by Oberon Books Ltd
521 Caledonian Road, London N7 9RH
Tel: +44 (0) 20 7607 3637 / Fax: +44 (0) 20 7607 3629
e-mail: info@oberonbooks.com
www.bloomsbury.com

A catalogue record for this book is available from the British
Library.

PB ISBN: 9781783194957
E ISBN: 9781783194964

Cover image by Stephen O'Neil

Visit www.bloomsbury.com to read more about all our books and
to buy them. You will also find features, author interviews and
news of any author events, and you can sign up for e-newsletters
so that you're always first to hear about our new releases.

Fever Dream: Southside was first performed at Citizens Theatre, Glasgow on 23 April 2015 with the following cast:

JULIA	Charlene Boyd
JOE 1	Martin Donaghy
KULDEV	Umar Malik
PETER	Martin McCormick
RAJ	Dharmesh Patel
JOE 2	Scott Reid
DEMI	Kirsty Stuart
TERRY	Harry Ward

Creative Team

Director	Dominic Hill
Designer	Neil Warmington
Lighting Designer	Lizzie Powell
Composer / Music Director	Michael John McCarthy
Puppet Designer / Maker	Gavin Glover
Sound Designer	Guy Coletta
Dramaturg	Frances Poet
Assistant Director	Stephen Darcy

A version of the first half of this play was presented by students of The Royal Conservatoire Scotland in August 2008. It played The Tron, Hampstead Theatre and The Traverse.

The project was developed and supported by The Playwrights Studio Scotland.

It was directed by Amanda Gaughan with sound design by Claire McKenzie. The actors were…Philip G Burke, Jeremy Crawford, Cindy Derby, Barbara Sullivan, Matthew McVarish and Amy Conway.

For Ellis

There is a massive neon sign.

It flickers on in racy porno red.

It's a Southside landmark.
Bolted to the sandstone
It hangs high
Above a bank
At the very heart of Victoria Road, Glasgow.

It says…

CHRIST
DIED
FOR OUR
SINS

It should be present throughout the play in one way or another…

ONE

A bare flat. A terrifying noise.

JOE TWO is in the living room. He's wearing a hooded top and jeans. He has a clean-cut collegiate look.

He doesn't seem too rattled by the mighty, floorboard-juddering shrieks and thumps coming from the other side of the bedroom door.

What the fuck is back there? Some kind of massive animal? Some kind of madman?

It roars. The furniture trembles.

Then…it goes suddenly quiet.

JOE TWO turns. Mm. That's unusual.

JOE TWO goes to the bedroom door and presses his ear against it. He's just about to open it when…

JOE ONE comes through the front door.

He is identically dressed, with the same well-combed-virgin vibe as JOE TWO. Physically though, they are poles apart.

JOE TWO moves away from the bedroom door guiltily. They are both in their late teens/early twenties and American.

JOE ONE: He's gone.

JOE TWO: For sure?

JOE ONE: His room's empty and Mrs Bell says she saw him walking towards town at six am. He was weeping Joe.

JOE TWO: That doesn't mean he's gone Joe.

JOE ONE: Joe, he's gone.

JOE TWO: Did you try calling him?

JOE ONE: Of course.

JOE TWO: That doesn't mean he's gone Joe.

JOE ONE: I called the States also.

JOE TWO: Okay.

JOE ONE: It's a different time over there so…

JOE TWO: But they answered right Joe? They're sending someone over right now to be our new Guide? Right? Or maybe they'll even issue a Deep Clean? Are they going to do a Deep Clean Joe, is that it?

JOE ONE decides to be the adult…

JOE ONE: Look I'll call again later. But you're right. They won't leave us here on our own.

JOE TWO: *(Points out the window.)* With the monsters.

JOE ONE: Joe, they're not monsters. They're people. Normal Scottish people. They're just like…

JOE TWO: *(Overlapping.)* 'They're just like children.' I know Joe. So we forgive them. Just like we would forgive a child.

JOE ONE: That's right Joe.

JOE TWO: But Joe. They're not children are they?

JOE ONE: No, they're *like* children.

JOE TWO: Because children aren't drunk all the time. Not normal children. I'm not sure you'd forgive a normal child if he were drunk all the time.

JOE ONE: These people aren't drunk all the time Joe.

JOE TWO: Nearly all the time. They growl Joe – worse than Terry. I can't understand a word they say. And so many Muslims Joe.

JOE ONE: I know.

JOE TWO: Everywhere! Monsters. *Like* monsters I mean. What happens if we're left here?

JOE ONE: We won't be… That's… We've just got to stay focused on the Gameplan. Okay? Nothing's changed Joe. Not really. In fact, it might even be better now. Without him. This trip is to test us. Yeah? To let us walk in the wilderness like Jesus in the desert. This is our desert Joe. This is all part of the test.

JOE TWO: *(Sarcastic.)* Oh yeah. You know what The Fathers are thinking. You've been called into the Media Room.

You've sat in front of those screens discussing Gameplans and Deep Cleans. Sure. This is all part of the test.

JOE ONE: All we can do is walk the street like we're supposed to. We walk the street, we speak to the people, we hand out the literature and we stand on doorsteps. One by one. Soul by soul.

JOE TWO: Monster by monster. We don't have any money do we Joe?

JOE ONE: *(Ignoring that.)* And when we get back tonight I'll call again and we'll get another Guide. It's not a big deal. Really. The Head Office is in…what?… Northington?

JOE TWO: Norville?

JOE ONE: Yeah. I left a message there too. So they'll be here in days. Maybe hours. Until then we should look at Victoria Road like it's a desert stretching out: lying there waiting, just for us. Our very own wilderness. Just like Jesus. Joe, think about it. Right now…we're not dissimilar to Jesus. Are we? Not really.

JOE TWO: Joe… Jesus met the Devil in the wilderness. The devil showed him a city. He said to Jesus, you can have this city if you want it.

JOE ONE: And Jesus turned him down Joe.

JOE TWO: Because he was getting the whole of heaven from God as a gift when he died on the cross! Who would want a city when they can have a heaven in the sky? It's a no-brainer. But we're not getting a heaven. Not after what…

JOE ONE: Oh Joe we are!

JOE TWO: Not of our *own*. Not to rule over as Kings, sitting at the right hand of our Father at the top table. We're there, sure, maybe – but we're way, way, way down at the bottom of the table. Maybe even on a separate table. Near the kitchen or…

JOE ONE: Joe…

JOE TWO: No Joe! Lookit. What if we go out there today, into the wilderness, alone, guideless… Monsters to the left of us, monsters to the right…and we meet the Devil? And what if he offers us a city? What then Joe?

# #

Another flat. A bedroom. The lights on a baby monitor rocket up into the red. The same shade of red as the CHRIST/SIN sign.

The sound of the baby crying is drowned out by the noise of a police helicopter and some shouting in the street.

PETER is peeking out the window watching some incident in the street. He's in his early thirties. He's all keyed up…wired and changeable. He feels ill.

His wife DEMI is the same age, but seems older somehow. Is it because, more often than not, she's the grown-up?

PETER: It's like fucking Compton this, man.

DEMI: Sssh. He's gone down.

PETER: *(He points out the window.)* Not for long. No one can sleep with that bloody thing buzzing away all the time like a… It's a sad day when your baby monitor is drowned out by the sounds of a police helicopter at…what time is it?… nine in the morning. Listening to his baby monitor is like listening to a fucking NWA album. I can't raise a child in this reality. I just can't do it. *(Feels his own forehead.)* Christ. I still feel shit by the way. Burning up.

DEMI: Compton's nice. We used to go there on holiday.

PETER: Different Compton.

DEMI: Ours was in Devon.

PETER: Aye, different Compton.

DEMI: You should lie down if you're feeling ill. I don't think he'll be quiet for long.

DEMI lies down but PETER doesn't.

PETER: *(Impassioned.)* Why doesn't he sleep?

DEMI: He's sleeping now.

He is. It's quiet.

PETER: We're doing something very wrong. Aren't we? He's not right.

DEMI: Sssh. He's okay. He's just teething.

PETER: I think he's got a kind of deep-rooted unrest. He's troubled. In his soul. We've got a troubled baby. He looks at me funny. Like he's saying… 'Do something you!'

DEMI takes a deep breath, she can't listen to this shit now.

DEMI: Are you remembering I'm out later?

PETER: No. Where?

DEMI: Helping set up the rally. I should be down there now but… I can't move. Could you tell them I'll be a bit late? Say we had a bad night.

PETER: Me?

DEMI: They need your soundscape in for today anyway. For the run through. You should show your face.

PETER: Ach. That's…that's a sinking ship. Community rally. What community? Look out the window. Plus, it's tomorrow. What's the sudden rush for everything? Let the other lazy bastards on the committee set it up. You do everything else. Spread sheets and all that. I don't even know why you're bothering.

DEMI: If I don't, who will? And it's tomorrow so we can get the girl's face seen. Flyers, banners…who knows. Might help jog some memories.

PETER: It's too late, Demi. She's been missing for days.

DEMI: Don't say that.

There's a noise in the street. PETER runs to the window and looks out.

PETER: Nothing. Just the gypsy kids.

DEMI: You don't say Gypsies.

PETER: Yeah, I know, but Eastern European sounds a bit…

DEMI: Gypsy Travellers. Or Romany. Or Roma or…

PETER: Yeah alright, alright. *(Forehead.)* Shit, man. I'm on fire here.

PETER picks up a guitar and strums it.

DEMI: I like the way they play.

PETER: Who?

DEMI: The Roma children.

PETER: Oh I don't. They unnerve me. They've got old faces.

DEMI: They play like I used to play. Out all day, just roaming the place in a dirty big troop, looking for fun. It's like Glasgow of yesteryear.

PETER: One of them begged me for money. Tell you that? Just out there. With the dad watching. Made me very uncomfortable. And they just move on too. They get to leave. It's not fair. We're solid and they're…whatever. I mean I'm all for immigration and that – a mix of cultures and stuff – but see once…one of those Traveller kids sprayed me with a can of Lynx when I had my arms full of shopping. With the dad watching! That's not on, man. I mean what happens when suddenly people turn up who don't play by the rules? In your bins and that, looking for something. I didn't ask to be stuck here. Christ. I wish I could drive.

PETER puts the guitar down and stands to get a better look at something. He's awful fidgety…

DEMI: Well, they always seem so glad to see me. It's nice. I let them push the pram.

PETER: *(Turning.)* What?!

DEMI: They love it.

PETER: Christ sake Demi, you can't just… They're Dickensian urchins in all but name. They…and I hate to say it cos it's – you know…but they steal things.

DEMI: I don't think they'll steal a pram with a baby in it Peter. God, you're so…

PETER: *(Overlapping.)* I'm not! Sensing danger is not the same as being scared.

Beat.

DEMI: So are we going to let wee Al play out in the streets? When he gets bigger. Or in the park?

PETER: Well. It won't be an issue will it?

DEMI: Why?

PETER: We'll be in the country by then.

DEMI: A nice little cottage in Compton?

PETER: Aye, out brambling with Ice Cube.

DEMI: And how do you suppose we'll be able to afford...?

PETER: Something will've come up and we'll've moved. That's what happens. You have a bit of a struggle when you first get married, the baby is born in a shithole, but then something comes up and you move somewhere nice. He'll be able to boast about it. Scottish people love to boast about their shite roots. There's nothing worse in this country than to come from a comfortable background. We actually feel sorry for people that went to private school. In fact I would go as far as to say that there are no middle-class people in Scotland. Well, none who would admit to being middle class anyway. So he'll thank us for this – we're giving him a very poor start – which is ideal. But yeah, in a few years it'll be the country, gardens, red wine on the decking – community. *(Beat and change.)* But fuck man, what if that doesn't happen? Think about it. *How* can it happen? Really? If we want to step up we're gonna have to get a hundred and fifty grand for this place at least and that's not happening. Unless your dad changes his will or something and gives us a deposit. But he won't. Will he? Can he? I mean, would they even let him, now he's mental?

DEMI: *(Getting tetchy.)* I don't know Peter. Why don't you ask him? Visiting is between two and four. While you're there you can thank him for paying our mortgage every month. But you won't will you? Cos you don't 'deal' with mortgages and deposits and money and spread sheets. You leave all that to me.

PETER: I can't visit him. He thinks I'm Satan. He says I'm going to open the gates of Hell.

DEMI: Doesn't mean he wouldn't appreciate a visit. *(Deep breath.)* It's up to us to make this place nice. Let's just get on with it.

PETER: Demi, if you think you can make this place nice you're as mental as your old boy.

DEMI: *(Snapping.)* Don't say that! Don't bloody say that! Even as a joke! It's not fucking funny Peter. Okay?

The baby starts to cry. They look at the baby monitor.

PETER: Do you think if I was in a coma people would say, 'Oh Peter will be alright – he's a fighter.' I don't think they would.

The police helicopter goes over again…

We're in Govanhill Baths, an Edwardian swimming pool which was closed and barricaded in 2001.

The puddles of water reflect the sunlight onto dirty tiles. Weird plants are climbing up the wall. It's daylight, but dark. It echoes. There is a gaping black drop, off into what was the pool itself.

There are piles of plastic chairs and tables and a big banner on the wall: 'SINK OR SWIM? COMMUNITY RALLY. GOVANHILL BATHS. WE SHALL RISE AGAIN!' There are also loads of MISSING PERSON placards stacked to the side, each showing a picture of a smiling girl in her twenties wearing a pink wig. A cardboard box full of flyers sits to the side.

KULDEV is alone, running through a speech he has printed on a piece of A4. He's sixteen, but in his Huchesons' Grammar School uniform he looks a lot younger. Even with no one listening he stammers and splutters. Not a natural public speaker. Nervous. He's trying – and failing – to learn these words…

KULDEV: *(Reading.)* 'I am... I am the voice of youth. The voice of youth. I am... I am the voice of the future...' Fuck. 'Youth. I am the future. I...am...in danger... I am in danger here...living here is no life for me...' Fuck sake! 'I am the... danger here...'

JULIA comes in with a heavy flight case. She's an artist in her late 20s. She's as clipped and odd as her haircut. In the past she worked hard to be kooky. She's beyond that now.

JULIA: Hey. You. Yes, you. Take this, yeah.

When KULDEV clocks that JULIA is talking to him he scuttles over to help her with the case. As soon as he has the slightest grip, JULIA leaves him to it and strides ahead, checking the place out. KULDEV follows her, struggling with the load...

JULIA: Jesus. Yeah. I pictured something more Gothic but, no...this is interesting. I've been resisting using this place, you know. The Studios are so full of people doing Govanhill Baths stuff: installations and prints and water pieces and blah blah blah... I had to fight that or be sucked under with that whole Bo-Ho Southside scene. I didn't even want to see inside. But, no, this is interesting. Abandoned. Yeah? Once there was joy here...health... childish shouts...but now what? I see dereliction, okay, but what else? Life. Yeah. These weeds, see? The jungle reclaiming its territory, dragging this place back to its primordial state. That's very usable. *(Breezy.)* Nah, I just thought fuck it man, the time is right. Know what I mean? Why resist it? So here I am. Plus, if it ever opened up again I could totally see myself swimming here and stuff. Unless it was popular. I need a two hour get-in and a private space. I don't want to be introduced though, I'll emerge organically throughout the evening.

KULDEV: Eh...em... I... I'm not... Raj is kinda...

JULIA: The contact I have is... *(Reads from her phone.)* 'Demi'? Are you Demi? I need a private space. It's not a Diva thing, it's to do with papier-mâché.

KULDEV: I'm Kuldev.

JULIA: And so Demi is…?

KULDEV: I dunno. I'm on work experience. For Raj. Bring down the leaflets he said. See. That's them. *(Doom.)* And eh… I've to make a speech too. Or something. But I don't think…

JULIA: *(Not interested.)* Oh right. God. Speeches. Well hopefully all the am-dram stuff will be done and dusted before I'm on. I'll speak to Demi. The 'we shall overcome' local collective thing is cool, you know, but I really think if they want this to be the start of something real for this place – something genuinely powerful – then they have to respect the professional artists involved. It's only when the artists move in that real change occurs. Everyone says that.

KULDEV: Are you an artist then?

JULIA: Well. Yeah. That limits it, but yeah. Okay.

KULDEV: And you're doing a show? Tomorrow at the rally?

JULIA: It's a piece.

KULDEV: What happens?

JULIA: What do you mean?

KULDEV: In your show. In your piece. What actually happens?

JULIA: Do you mean figuratively?

KULDEV: Em…well…eh… I was just wondering… what, like, actually happens in your show?

JULIA: *(Laughs. For ages.)* I don't really know how you want me to answer that question. I'd have to illustrate.

KULDEV: Oh right. Sorry.

JULIA: I don't think of my pieces in terms of 'things happening'. I don't think anyone does nowadays.

KULDEV: Right. But do you speak? Out loud I mean. To the crowd?

JULIA: There can be text.

KULDEV: *(A little harder.)* But do you speak?

JULIA: I've just said. Text is an option. I can illustrate.

JULIA starts unpacking her flight case...

KULDEV watches her. Eventually...almost to himself...

KULDEV: It's just... I'm meant to be doing this speech, right? Raj wrote it. But... I dunno... I just... I don't want to. I can't. I can't speak.

JULIA: *(Absently, as she looks through her stuff for something.)* Yeah, well, don't sweat it. Honestly. No one can speak nowadays. These politicians right...the ones that'll be here tomorrow night...they can't speak either. They want power but they can't perform. It's mad. Everyone knows that real power *comes* from performance. The performance comes first, man! *(Long suffering sigh.)* I wish they would just ask for my help, but they never do. Ever. I'd tell them. I'd say, 'speak with passion...with words we can understand... visualise the communion of the piece and actuate'! I mean, my god. How hard is that? But they're all petrified. If they could speak...if they could perform...they'd go through this city like a hot knife through butter. And talking about hot knives...

JULIA has found what she's looking for...a huge, medieval-looking dagger...she starts some music playing on her phone...

JULIA: Check this out.

JULIA slits her throat. Blood is sprayed all over the place – all over KULDEV.

He screams.

JULIA drops to the floor. Dead.

The JOES' flat. Continuing the previous scene...

JOE ONE: Maybe we should try to pray *together* this morning?

JOE TWO: Hey, what were you two talking about last night Joe?

JOE ONE: Nothing.

JOE TWO: You were talking about bodies. I heard you Joe. It's…

JOE ONE: *(Overlapping.)* Being honest.

JOE TWO: *(Overlapping.)* Very worrying. Okay, okay. Being honest then – is that why Brother Kyle left? Is that why there's weeping at 6am and why we're left here, guideless? Honestly? Bodies, bodies, bodies?

JOE ONE: We were…it was a conversation about…it was…we were talking about temptation.

JOE TWO: Again?

The Govanhill baths. KULDEV and JULIA, following straight on…

KULDEV stands over JULIA's body, blood pooling around the knife.

RAJ enters, texting.

RAJ is a very sharp-looking young man in an expensive suit and tie. He's in his early thirties and is aiming for the calm self-possession of a top sportsman or a TV mobster. He only just falls short. There's a chink of daylight in his manner that softens him.

RAJ doesn't see JULIA.

KULDEV: Raj! I… I…

RAJ: *(Looking up from his phone. Seeing the box.)* For fuck sake! Don't tell me. Don't fucking tell me…are those the flyers from this morning?!

KULDEV: Eh…

RAJ: How many times? Those flyers get handed out in Queens Park! Am I gonna have to chin you to get my point across?

KULDEV: No, I…it's just the speech has got me all kinda…

RAJ: *(Taking the piss.)* 'The speech has got me all kinda…' I was told you were crème de la crème, Twinkle. Huchesons' finest. *(Easier.)* By the way, here's a good bit of mentoring for you, write this down: see if you *are* gonna get chinned it's best to imagine you're a prizefighter and getting chinned is a normal occurrence. The imagination prepares the reality. Know what I mean? Are you listening to music? What is this, The Cure?

RAJ finally sees JULIA.

There's a big, stunned pause before...

JULIA springs to her feet, twisting and dancing. The men are startled.

JULIA: Resurrection, baby. I am reborn! Again and again she is reborn...

RAJ: What's...what...?

KULDEV: This is Julia. She's doing a piece at the thing tomorrow.

JULIA: Not Julia. Not in death. In death I am Lulu.

JULIA's doing some physical theatre moves now.

JULIA: Lulu is a ghost who wanders the streets of the Southside. Unseen. Unloved. Unliving. But all knowing. Lulu cannot rest until she finds the end of her story. Lulu's story is made from found fragments, moments of connection between strangers...

RAJ: How the fuck is that the Lulu story?

JULIA: Different Lulu. Lulu finds her storyteller. She selects a member of the audience...

She takes KULDEV's hand and pulls him towards her. She dances with him...

JULIA: They dance. And as they dance they remember. Something in Lulu's movement, her touch, provokes a deep sense of memory in the dancer – if not a literal memory itself – which then leads to a testimony.

KULDEV: What do you want me to do?

JULIA: Nothing. This isn't the piece. This is the illustration. In the piece the audience member will tell us something he has long since forgotten. A little story about living in Govanhill. And with the memory, Lulu is banished...the ghost dies...and...at long last... Julia returns...

JULIA coils back to the floor. She waits for a few beats (maybe a touch too long.) before she gets up and dusts herself off. All business now…

JULIA: Thanks. Obviously it's faked. I have to use a stooge to do the memory, but it's remarkably interesting. *(To RAJ.)* Are you Demi? I need a private space and a two hour get in.

The helicopter buzzes over.

# #

Back in DEMI and PETER's room. Following on… The baby is quiet and PETER's looking out the window.

DEMI: I'm thinking of going back to church.

PETER: What? Why?

DEMI: Why do you think?

PETER: What, cos they're happy? Well they're not, Demi. They're delusional. There's a difference. Let me tell you something about religion…the suicide bomber screaming 'God is great' on the school bus is in the same gang as the old lady doing the coffee morning round the corner – the bomber just believes in it more. It's all connected.

DEMI: Oh shut up Peter.

PETER: Or is this…em… all about whatisname… Raj Singh The Slumlord? Just cos he's bringing down a busload from The Temple you want to even up the numbers with some Christian faces? That it?

DEMI: *(Sarcastic.)* Yeah that's it Peter. I want to get a nice mix of faiths for the photo op.

PETER: That kind of shit totally goes against my principles.

DEMI: And what are they again? I can't keep up. When we first met you were Christian Union boy, then you were a Buddhist with all those little flags and now you're a Dawkins disciple. Or you would be if you could finish any of his books.

PETER: *(Stung.)* Well…so? When we first met you wore stilettos.

DEMI: And those heels wore down. If you must know, I just fancied talking about something *big* for a change. Something bigger than streets. And crime rates. And spreadsheets.

PETER: Are you only going to get away from me?

DEMI: *(Unconvincing.)* No.

PETER: To get away from wee Al?

DEMI: What? No! Shut up Peter. Look, I need to sleep. Go and tell them I'll be late and hand your soundscape in to that artist woman. Please.

PETER: I'm working today.

DEMI: You don't open up for an hour.

PETER: Thing is…see the soundscape…?

DEMI: It's not finished. I know. We're all very surprised.

PETER: Don't say it like that. I've been busy at work.

DEMI: You do two shifts at the Oxfam Record and Book shop. How busy can that get?

PETER: And I happen to be a stay-at-home dad, Demi. In case you haven't noticed.

DEMI: You stayed at home long before you were a dad, Peter. I never expected it to be finished. You've never finished anything. It doesn't matter. Just hand it in. It'll do.

Beat.

PETER: I thought you liked that about me though? My thingme. Laidbackness.

DEMI: You mean the fact that you tinker? You dabble? You have hobbies but no occupation? That you have never finished a damn thing in your entire life? You thought I found that attractive?

(Beat.)

PETER: *(Weakly.)* Yeah.

DEMI: Well I don't. No one does. Keys.

DEMI picks up a big set of shop keys and chucks them at PETER. He catches them.

The helicopter buzzes again…

# #

JOE and JOE. Where we left them.

JOE TWO: I think we should bring Terry with us.

JOE ONE: *(Touchy subject.)* No Joe.

JOE TWO: Just for today. We'll be alone out there Joe!

JOE ONE: No Joe.

JOE TWO: He can protect us. He can show those monsters who's…

JOE ONE: *(Overlapping.)* We've been over it and over it. Brother Kyle said…

JOE TWO: Brother Kyle has abandoned us!

Beat.

JOE ONE: *(Whispering.)* Joe c'mon man. Terry puts people off. You know it. Folks don't wanna invite us in if we have Terry with us.

JOE TWO: He's awful sick Joe. He's gone quiet. I think he's going to die.

JOE ONE: Well…

JOE TWO: He needs to get out of here.

JOE ONE: No Joe.

JOE TWO: He's one of God's miracles Joe. People need to see Terry.

JOE ONE: I know Joe.

JOE TWO: I'm scared of what he's going to do if we don't…

JOE ONE: I know! And that's another reason why he should stay in his room, for now, with the door locked. Don't… don't open that door Joe.

Govanhill Baths. RAJ, KULDEV and JULIA, where we left them…

RAJ: So, let me just make sure I understand this right…you're going to do a show at the rally tomorrow – a rally designed to illustrate that the community can pull together and that Govanhill is nice – which involves you slitting your own throat with a fake knife and spraying fake blood all over the shop?

JULIA: That's a component, yeah. What, are you outraged? Shocked? Great art challenges. I'm sorry, but I won't apologise for that.

RAJ: And Demi's okayed this has she?

JULIA: I'm not asking for permission.

RAJ: But does Demi even know what…?

JULIA: Look I'm sure that this 'Demi' will see that what I'm doing is fore-fronting notions of memory and rebirth through live art performance methods. It's a very positive message.

RAJ: Yeah, I wouldn't bet your mortgage on it. She's a fascist dressed up as liberal. There's loads of them.

JULIA: *(Wobbling slightly.)* Well. I'm not afraid of confrontation. And anyway it's not like there's been a knife crime recently or anything. *(Unsure.)* Has there?

RAJ: *(Sarcastic.)* What in Glasgow? Doubt it. No, my guess is she'll say it's in bad taste, what with that girl gone missing, but hey – I've been wrong before.

JULIA: It's unconnected. I didn't know there was a girl missing. I deliberately don't watch the news so reality can't contaminate my work. Honestly! I don't even know her name or her age or what she looked like or anything, so frankly, I don't see how you can stand there and say I'm being exploitative.

RAJ: *(Holds his hands up in surrender. Smiling.)* I'm saying nothing. Tell Demi I showed my face. As promised. Twinkle. Grab those flyers and let's get this done. Finally.

KULDEV grabs the box of flyers and goes to exit with RAJ. RAJ has a thought…

RAJ: *(To JULIA.)* FYI. The missing girl is called Isabelle Kennedy. Goes by Izzy. She's twenty-five years old. Sang in a band. And she looks like that. Hard to miss eh? Keep on keeping on, Lulu. I'm loving your work.

RAJ hands JULIA a flyer.

RAJ: Onwards Twinkle! Onwards!

RAJ exits singing 'Shout' by Lulu.

KULDEV follows. Then he stops and turns to JULIA…

KULDEV: It works, by the way. I feel a little different.

KULDEV runs off.

The helicopter buzzes overhead…

#

PETER and DEMI, following on. PETER is getting ready to go – coat on and pulling a memory stick from a laptop…

PETER: We should have sex again. At some point. That might help.

DEMI: I know. But not now.

PETER: Oh God no, not now. Jesus.

DEMI: Look. I'm sorry I snapped at you. I'm just tired.

PETER: Yeah. Me too. Cannae shake this bloody headache man.

DEMI: It will all go away, don't worry.

PETER: What? My temperature? Aye. It's been ages though. Since the wee man was born. Doctor says…

DEMI: No, I mean this *time*. This time will go away. It's just a phase. Look, maybe the soundscape will go down a bomb tomorrow and this'll be the start of something?

PETER: What? Record companies? Is that what you're saying? Use it as a showcase for any A&R guys that might pop in or something?

DEMI: Well… I think it's pretty unlikely any A&R guys'll pop in. But just *doing* something. With people. That risky, nervous feeling. That might get you alive again.

There's the sound of a deep animal bark, or growl, from somewhere in the street. They both notice it. They go to the window and have a wee look, but can't spot anything. After a bit…

PETER: I don't know if I can protect him from all these noises.

DEMI: They're just noises.

PETER: Christ. I hope that girl turns up.

JULIA is alone in the baths. Following on…

She glances at the flyer in her hand. She sees, for the first time, the photo of the victim…

It's as if she has been punched. She's staring wildly at the flyer, she's gasping for air. She thinks she's going to faint…

JULIA: Is this… Is this a fucking joke? *(Shouting.)* Is this a fucking joke!?

JULIA grabs her bag and knife – leaving the flight case – and runs out of the pool, stumbling, still clutching the flyer.

In PETER and DEMI's flat following on.

DEMI picks up the baby monitor and has a quick look…

DEMI: 25 degrees. Christ, that is hot. I should've just put him in a vest.

PETER: Hey, what do you mean, 'get me alive again?'

DEMI: Ach, I just mean…

There is an almighty, otherworldly, <u>shriek</u> from the baby monitor.

It crescendos into a massive, wall-trembling roar.

PETER screams and DEMI drops the baby monitor

PETER is frozen. Petrified.

DEMI runs off to the baby's room.

PETER: What is it!? What is it!!!!?

A horrible few moments for PETER…alone.

Eventually DEMI returns holding the baby. Her heart is pounding but the baby is fine.

After a few moments…

PETER: What was it?

DEMI: I don't know. Nothing. Must've been something outside his window.

PETER comes over and they hold each other, so relieved they're laughing.

PETER: Fucking shat myself man.

DEMI: Everything's all right. It was only a big, scary noise. Everything's all right.

For a moment they form a happy, almost holy-family tableau.

But PETER can't hold it. He has to go to the window for a look to see if he can see whatever the hell made that sound.

JOE and JOE get down on their knees to pray. They hold hands…

JOE TWO: I love you Joe.

JOE ONE: I love you Joe.

The sound of the police helicopter and some shouting in the street moves time on…

TWO

The same day. Later on.

RAJ and KULDEV are up at the flagpole in Queens Park. Glasgow is the vista behind them.

KULDEV is handing out the flyers from the box. RAJ is sitting on a park bench eating tablet from a poke. KULDEV seems to have a little more steel in him. He's still on the bounce from his dance with JULIA.

RAJ: Know what my Dad said the other day? He said the Govanhill Baths were the 'greatest community regeneration project in Europe'. *(Shakes his head in disbelief.)* You may be tempted to consider that an attempt at humour, but trust me, the guy doesn't do jokes. You can't be as religious as he is and funny – they cancel each other out. In my opinion, the sooner those baths are converted into flats the better. *(Standing up and taking in the view.)* God it's ugly sure it is?

KULDEV: What? Govanhill Baths?

RAJ: The whole thing. Glasgow is an ugly, ugly city.

KULDEV: Some of it's nice.

RAJ: That's what they always say. But if I gave you a sandwich and said, 'here try this, some of it's nice', would you eat it?

A beat or two. KULDEV is losing his patience with all this…

KULDEV: Then…why are we doing it?

RAJ: Doing what?

KULDEV: This! Why are we in the park handing out flyers about a missing girl and helping with a community rally? If you hate the place so much why am I…bloody…making a speech?

RAJ: You're making a speech, Twinkle, because you're the Voice of Youth.

KULDEV: But *why* am I the Voice of Youth?

RAJ: Because I told you to be the Voice of Youth.

KULDEV: This is supposed to be work experience though.

RAJ: This *is* work experience.

KULDEV: I'm supposed to learning about Property Management.

RAJ: Why the hell would you want to learn about Property Management?

KULDEV: Because you're a Property Manager!

RAJ: That doesn't answer the question.

KULDEV: I'm… I… I'm not doing it. Okay? I'm not speaking. I'm just not. I can't. I won't. You actually can't make me.

RAJ straightens. He is stony faced.

KULDEV: And…em…you know…apart from anything else, it's not very nice. The speech. *(He gets the speech out of his pocket.)* It's scaremongering. I know you wrote it and maybe you imagined it being said in a certain way, but see to me, it sends the wrong message: that young people are frightened. Trapped. That we're all victims here. It paints a very bleak and unrepresentative picture of the area. Plus I stutter when I'm nervous as well. So. That's that. Not happening. Decided.

Big pause. RAJ stares at KULDEV. KULDEV seems a little different now right enough. A little rougher round the edges.

KULDEV: And? Am I supposed to be intimidated? Well, guess what? No. No!

KULDEV rips up the speech. He throws it on the ground.

RAJ smiles.

RAJ: Tablet, Twinkle?

KULDEV: My name's not Twinkle. It's Kuldev.

RAJ: My mistake. Sorry. Tablet, Twinkle?

A standoff.

KULDEV puts his hand in the bag and RAJ squeezes his hand painfully…

KULDEV: Ahhhh!

RAJ: *(Breezy.)* Here, talking about speeches that aren't very nice. Check this out…

RAJ gets out his phone. After a few taps and scrolls he finds what he's looking for…

RAJ: Are we sitting comfortably? Then I'll begin. Ahem… *(Reading.)* 'My father, my uncles, my cousins. Absent. Failures. Weak…'

KULDEV: What…? Where did you get that?

RAJ: *(Cont.)* '… I know… I am certain… I am not like them. I will never be. They cannot teach me a fucking thing…' Tut tut tut. Terrible language in one so young.

KULDEV: How did you get that?!

RAJ: *(Reading.)* 'Political leaders, cultural leaders, celebrities– my so-called role models. They are useless and despicable to me. The country ages and gets poorer by the day. The streets are filled with walking corpses, diddy neds and fake-tanned fatties. Phonies, weaklings and children. So I say to myself, "Where are the Big Dogs? Where are the Players at a World Level to lift me up upon their shoulders?" They do not exist. Not here. There are no Men in this city. In this country. We just stopped making them. Like we stopped making battleships. And so we will never win another war. I want to be a Big Dog. I want real power. I want to be… an Emperor. And if the weak must be swept into oblivion to make that happen…then so be it.'

Pause as RAJ looks at KULDEV. KULDEV is stunned and flustered…

KULDEV: That's…that was private. No one was meant to see that.

RAJ: Oh your poor mother. What a shock she got when she came across it, as she was innocently raking through your hard drive. Sounds like extremist talk, she thought to herself, tears in her eyes…

KULDEV: I'm not an extremist…

RAJ: She runs to my father in Temple: 'Oh Mr Singh, save my boy from a mugshot and a jumpsuit!'

KULDEV: It was…it was an essay… I…

RAJ: Pillar of the community my old man. As you know. Normally you'd be getting the famous Sonny Singh 'Calm Down Son' lecture. But the thing is…it kinda rang a bell for him. All this stuff…your 'essay'…well… My dad knew someone who used to say things just like that.

KULDEV: Who?

RAJ: Me. We're peas in a pod, Twinkle. Not least because we're…you know…?

KULDEV: What?

RAJ: English!

KULDEV: So?

RAJ: So…it's a sign! We're the same! In Glasgow, you and me, we're on the outside looking in. We've got to smash that glass or we'll freeze to death, man. Course, I made a mistake. I smashed it too early. Got myself expelled from school. Had to build a new act from scratch. Now my dad sees me as a success story…the bad boy with crazy ideas, who changed his ways and got straight and respectable. So he asked me… 'Can you do the same for this kid? Take him under your wing and mentor him to righteousness.' But what Dad doesn't know is… I didn't change. Actually… I got worse. I put those crazy ideas into practice. And now I'm looking for an apprentice. I'm looking to do for my mentee what my father never did for me. I want to give this kid a shot at 'real power'. And if the weak must be swept into oblivion to make that happen…so be it.

KULDEV: So…you're not a property manager?

RAJ: Property management is but a street name in the atlas of what I do, Twinkle. But it's not my title.

KULDEV: What's your title?

RAJ: I am…an Oligarch.

A beat.

Then KULDEV bursts out laughing.

We're in JULIA's workspace in Southside Studios, minutes from Govanhill Baths. The usual artist-studio stuff – paint splatter, canvases, half-done sculptures, photos ripped from magazines on a 'blood' theme; nothing impressive or finished – but there are laptops and cameras and hi-tech gear in here too. Her bag from earlier is sitting next to the laptop. Her Lulu costume hangs on the wall...a red dress and a pink wig. The door is jammed shut with a chair.

JULIA is on the floor, staring at the flyer intensely. She's scared.

The door thuds. Someone's trying to get in. JULIA jumps. The handle rattles. JULIA scuttles into the corner.

After a beat or two there's a knock. Then a voice from the other side. It's PETER.

JULIA: Who is it?

PETER: Me. Peter. I'm from Demi. I'm her hingme. Husband. Are you Julia?

> *JULIA looks at the flyer again. Actually, a second opinion might be advisable here. After a beat or two to summon the courage, she kicks the chair away and PETER comes in.*

PETER: Were you using a chair to block the door there? I thought that only happened on television. *(Holding up the memory stick.)* I tried the baths but there's no one there. Demi said you worked in the Southside Studios, so I thought I'd give it a bit of the old detective shit. *(Awkward silence.)* I'm Demi's husband. This is my soundscape. It's kinda retro-grandiose Indie with a crescendo-y thing going on in the middle. Bit Mogwai-y. Some folk say it's like a Lego-pop version of *Disintegration*-era Cure, but I'm like that, no way. *(Sees her.)* What's up?

JULIA: Tell Demi it's off. Tomorrow. The...em...the integrity of the piece has been compromised.

PETER: Oh right. So...you don't need the soundscape?

JULIA: No. Sorry.

PETER: I think she's em…I think you're on the posters though.

JULIA: I can't perform. I can't be Lulu.

PETER: How come?

JULIA: Because I've gone missing.

PETER: Eh?

She hands PETER the flyer.

PETER: What's this?

JULIA: That's the girl they're looking for. That's Izzy Kennedy.

PETER: Yeah I know. So?

JULIA: That's me. That's a picture of me.

In the close of a tenement building on Albert Ave. Lots of noises from within and above…

JOE ONE is waiting outside a door which is trying its hardest to rise above its surroundings. There's a fake plant in a pot by the mat and a brass name plate. It's a shame that the felt pen graffiti on the wall attracts the eye. It says 'IRA'. And 'Don't screw the nut, nut the screw!!!'

JOE ONE is wondering about this last one (what does it mean?) when JOE TWO arrives, puffing up the stairs, carrying a bag from Greggs…

JOE ONE: Joe where have you been?

JOE TWO is harassed. He hands JOE ONE a sausage roll from his Greggs bag.

JOE TWO: I've been confronting monsters.

JOE ONE: Joe where have you…?

JOE TWO: Well firstly, I had to queue in the street for this.
That, I'll never get. Why do the monsters crave this stuff to the point that they will queue in the rain…and then it's not even hot. They're told 'it's not hot' and the monsters say 'oh that's fine'.

JOE ONE: But Joe you've been gone forty-five minutes. I've been standing here, paused.

JOE TWO: Listen Joe. Things have occurred.

JOE ONE: Oh.

JOE TWO: Major incidents.

JOE ONE: Can you remember them?

JOE TWO: Oh yeah.

JOE ONE: Can you tell me about them?

JOE TWO: You're not going to like it Joe. You're going to pinch your eyes and shake your head slowly. You're going to sigh and say 'well, this is something else'.

JOE ONE: I think you should tell me anyway Joe.

JOE TWO: I was stopped by a police officer in the park.

JOE ONE: Joe…

JOE TWO: He said he had some questions to ask me. So I got really, really…

JOE ONE: Scared…

JOE TWO: *(Simultaneously.)* Angry. And I started arguing and saying that now is not the time for accusation! Now is the time for calm reflection! I was screaming at him: 'Calm reflection! Calm reflection!'

JOE ONE: Oh no Joe. And then what happened?

JOE TWO: Well, then he said something into his radio and tried to take hold of my arm.

JOE ONE: Oh no Joe. Oh no.

JOE TWO: Yeah, so I just pushed him off and I ran away.

Beat.

JOE ONE: You ran away?

JOE TWO: Yeah.

JOE ONE: You…why Joe?

JOE TWO: Well, why was that police officer grabbing me Joe? There's an unusual atmosphere out there, Joe. Asking innocent people questions is not helping. Not one bit.

Pause. JOE ONE has to think.

JOE ONE: I think we need to go back there…

JOE TWO: No! That's the worst thing to do.

JOE ONE: That's what Jesus would do Joe.

JOE TWO: I disagree Joe. I think Jesus would be in a similar mood to when he attacked the money lenders in the temple. He'd be in his table-tipping mood.

JOE ONE: Joe, I just think…wait. Why were you in the park?

JOE TWO: I went back to the apartment, Joe. I was worried. Terry was quiet when we left and he hadn't eaten.

JOE ONE: Oh no Joe.

JOE TWO: This is actually the major incident. What I'm going to say now – this is where you pinch your eyes and…

JOE ONE: Joe, tell me you didn't open his door?

JOE TWO: I had to Joe. I'd bought him a steakbake.

JOE ONE: I thought you said…?

JOE TWO: Look Joe, I'm gonna be honest with you. I have, on occasion, taken Terry out of his room. I take him on my walks sometimes. In the park. But I always make sure to lock his door and bolt his window. I always do.

JOE ONE: So wait, you went back to the apartment to give him the steakbake and..?

JOE TWO: He's gone Joe. Terry's gone.

JULIA and PETER. Southside Studios. Following on.
PETER is looking at the flyer, confused. JULIA is pacing the room, wired…

PETER: But…you're not Izzy Kennedy. Are you?

JULIA: That's irrelevant. I knew I'd get disappeared someday and now it's happened.

PETER: Yeah, but…you haven't disappeared. Or have you? No. Couldn't've. You're here right now. Talking to me. Sure you are?

JULIA: Am I? How can you be sure?

A beat for that to freak PETER out a little bit…

JULIA: When I was a kid, I thought that every killer on the loose was out there hunting for me. *(Miles from laughter.)* It's hilarious actually. I would see clues in all the news reports…the victim had the same surname or the same hair colour or the same interests as me. He was working his way towards me, yeah? It was just a matter of time before the Killer Man vanished me for good.

PETER: *(The flyer.)* This isn't you though. This is Izzy Kennedy.

JULIA: Look at it. Look at it!

PETER: Okay. She looks a *wee* bit like you. Kind've.

JULIA: A wee bit?

PETER: It's quite similar, but…

JULIA: I've never forgotten The Killer Man. He's always been there. Worse now that I'm artist. When a new piece would die on the vine or when a show flopped or I'd botch another project – I could feel him coming towards me: The Killer Man coming closer and closer the worse I'd get, desperate to turn me invisible. He's been very, very close, for a long, long time. It's my theme. Look. *(Her art.)* And now… *(Holding up the flyer.)* It's over. My work is so bad that I'm not just a goner… I'm gone.

PETER: Em. Aye. Look. It's probably just a hingme. And you shouldn't say your work's bad. According to Demi folk say it's ace.

JULIA: No, they say it's 'interesting'. Which is what people say when they don't give a fuck. I'm a fake. I've been a fake for years. So now I'm… I'm a phantom.

PETER: Yeah. I'm probably not the best one to talk to about this to be honest. I've not been feeling very well recently. Plus I don't sleep, so my mind's all… My jammas were pure ringing this morning. With sweat I mean, not piss. But…em… I think you should just ignore all this 'vanishing' stuff and do the rally. It could be a showcase. A&R guys. Or something.

JULIA: Ignore it? I don't exist anymore!

Pause.

PETER: Have you been online?

JULIA shakes her head.

PETER: We could go online? Sometimes it helps.

A beat. Then JULIA nods and points to her laptop – she can't face it. PETER flicks it open and taps away…

PETER: Okay. Same picture. But your name's not Izzy Kennedy is it? That's established.

JULIA: My mother's name was Isabelle. My Granny's maiden name was Kennedy.

PETER: Yeah, but your name's not…

JULIA: Look at the picture! She was twenty-five. I'm twenty-five. We're the same.

PETER: *(Reading from the screen.)* Well… Says she was last seen walking through the park at 8.15pm on Friday night. What were you doing, quarter past eight, Friday?

JULIA: Walking through the park.

Beat.

PETER: She was wearing a short red dress and a pink wig.

JULIA groans. She points to the dress and wig hanging on the wall.

PETER: Well. Em. Okay. She was on her way back from a party?

JULIA: It was the launch of a pop-up gallery in Battlefield. There was nobody there but me. I told the owner the space wouldn't work – there was an absence of soul. The evening had a tang to it, I could smell summer coming, I cut through the park, I lit a joint...

PETER: Then what?

JULIA has to sit down. She's taking deep breathes just to stay conscious.

Big pause.

PETER is at a loss.

PETER: Do you want to hear my soundscape?

# #

The two JOES. Following on...

JOE ONE: What?

JOE TWO: Prepare yourself Joe. Terry's gone. I mean, *gone*. Someone turned that key. Someone opened that window. But who?

Pause. After a few beats to think this through, JOE ONE actually looks relieved. Happy even...

JOE ONE: Well...this is...good.

JOE TWO: What?

JOE ONE: This is good news Joe. This is a step forward.

JOE TWO: But Joe, he's gone.

JOE ONE: You went into his room?

JOE TWO: Yeah.

JOE ONE: And you couldn't see him?

Beat.

JOE TWO: Oh... I get it. I get what's going on here.

JOE ONE: *(Continuing.)* You couldn't see any sign of him? Not a trace?

JOE TWO: I can't believe you're doing this to me Joe...

JOE ONE: I'm just saying...

JOE TWO: I know what you're saying and it's arrogant.

JOE ONE: It's not arrogant.

JOE TWO: It *is* arrogant. Just like in our training: 'people who are in the darkness and use science for light are arrogant'.

JOE ONE: I'm not arrogant Joe. I'm just saying…

JOE TWO: What you are saying Joe is that I'm crazy. Right? And I gotta tell you, coming from you of all people that's kinda hard to swallow.

JOE ONE: What do you mean?

JOE TWO: Oh nothing. Just that… You think I don't know what you did back home? Maybe you can't remember Joe, but I can. Ever thought that the only reason you're an Angel on this International Growth Mission is because they wanted you on the other side of the world while they did a Deep Clean?

JOE ONE: What? I…

JOE TWO: I love you Joe, but I'm an old fashioned guy. Anyone else would've contacted the Fathers days ago, and told them that you're talking about bodies again and you're scaring away Brother Kyle and you're losing your faith. I know what's next. Headaches. Numb hands. Blackouts. Waking up with…

JOE ONE: That's not happening.

JOE TWO: Not yet. But I was told to watch for the warning signs and I'm worried.

JOE ONE: I'm not losing my faith.

JOE TWO: Well, you sound very like someone who is losing their faith. And that's a warning sign. You're talking like someone who believes in 'evolution'. Someone who would rather read fairy tales than the word of the Lord. Warning sign. What's next? Is the violence coming again, Joe? All that blood? Bodies, bodies, bodies. Are you a man or are you a monster, Joe? We'll see.

JOE ONE: I still believe.

JOE TWO: But not in Terry?

Pause.

JOE ONE: *(Carefully.)* Joe. Terry…is a pterodactyl.

JOE TWO: So?

# #

RAJ and KULDEV following on. KULDEV is still laughing…

RAJ: Do you even know what an Oligarch is?

KULDEV: Yeah.

RAJ: Do you though?

KULDEV: Of course I know what an Oligarch is! Everyone knows what an Oligarch is. You're not an Oligarch. How can a grubby little property manager on the Southside of Glasgow be an Oligarch? It's preposterous.

RAJ: Oh is that right? Preposterous? Do you know how much property I own within three miles of where we're standing right now? And do you know how much I'm *gonna* own? I'll tell you… All of it! *All* of it, Twinkle! As the Oligarchs bought bankrupt Russia, I want to buy – I'm *going* to buy – the Southside in its *entirety*. Every single last fucking bit of it. How about that for Big Dog ambition? And I tell you something else, I'm going to buy it cheap. I need those prices to plummet. I need the area to get *worse*. Cos when it hits rock bottom – like the Oligarch I am – I'll snap it all up. Snap!

A pause. KULDEV is, despite himself, beginning to take this seriously.

KULDEV: Okay. Maybe. Even if that *is* what you *think* you're doing, I have to go back to my first question… How come I'm the bloody Voice of Youth? Isn't stuff like that helping the area to…?

RAJ: *(Interrupting.)* No. The exact opposite. It's instigation, Twinkle. Instigation.

KULDEV: Which means…?

RAJ: See…we Oligarchs deal in no man's land. Grey areas. Disputed territories. That's how we trade and that's how we think. Morally, it's…complex. I need the property prices right across the Southside to slide. Sometimes that happens on its own and sometimes it needs a little push. After all, David Cameron's austerity drive can take us only so far.

KULDEV: So. Wait a minute. You're saying you actually do stuff…you take action…deliberate action…which makes the Southside worse?

RAJ: Instigation. Your speech is a part of that. A terrifying glimpse of a scared generation and a violent future for all concerned. And yeah, I won't deny, in this case it's a little personal. The woman that's running the rally owns a place in Albert Avenue. I've got every other flat in that close. If she would just sell hers to me it would be my first full house, so to speak. But she will not fucking budge. The wilder I make the close, the more determined she is to stay. She's making it 'nice'. People with babies work at that like slaves on a galley ship. I fucking hate her. So anything I can do to fuck up her attempt at local harmony the better. Two birds. Know what I mean?

KULDEV doesn't know what to make of this. Is it bullshit, or something important?

KULDEV: So…What do you do? How do you 'instigate'?

RAJ: Varies. *(He's proud of this.)* Like, you know how sometimes you'll see new-build flats and there'll be a million For Sale signs plastered over them, and you think, 'Christ, I wonder what's wrong with that joint?'

KULDEV: Mm.

RAJ: That's me! There's probably only one real sign in the whole bunch. I've just turned up in the middle of the night and stuck all the others up everywhere I can. Watch the prices tumble, man. *(A list.)* I run a fleet of vandals. I bomb out shops. I set up hell-bent house parties in nice areas that bang on for days and days. I'm actually working on a race riot now that I reckon is going to be my masterpiece. Sometimes all I'm doing is giving reality a wee nudge. Like that crazy artist cow earlier on. 'Yeah, on you go love...slit your throat at a community rally...fight the power!' Every little helps.

KULDEV: And it's illegal. All of this, right?

RAJ: Ach...it's illegal-*ish*. But I'm careful. Thing is though, it's exhausting. And who can I tell? I've been totally craving a mentee. Then your essay fell into my lap and I thought...oi oi. He'll do. So what do you say?

KULDEV: To what?

RAJ: Are you in? There's so much money to be made here it's terrifying. Think about it...owner's boxes...art dealerships...private planes...it's all for the fucking taking. We buy but we're never bought. We sell but we never get sold. Kuldev...you want 'real power'? This is it, man. You just had the wrong word. You said Emperor. But you meant Oligarch.

The JOES, following on...

JOE ONE: Joe, there are no pterodactyls. Not anymore.

JOE TWO: Oh so you've seen every corner of God's earth have you Joe...?

JOE ONE: No. Of course...

JOE TWO: Explored every island, every volcano, every forest? You know, for a fact, that there's not some hidden micro-climate that has lost, rare creatures like Terry which will prove, once and for all, that evolution is just a stab in the dark, just graffiti on the wall of time? You know more than God is that what you're saying?

JOE ONE: I'm not saying that...

JOE TWO is really angry now and rings the doorbell with attitude.

JOE TWO: So what are you saying then Joe? Are you saying that I've imagined Terry? Is that it? I've imagined a huge, dying pterodactyl, who coughs great piles of black phlegm on Mrs Bell's carpets have I? Are you saying I'm crazy? *I'm* the crazy one! Oh yeah Joe, *I'm* the one that's crazy. That's funny.

JOE ONE: But… Joe… You're the only person who's ever seen Terry.

JOE TWO: *(Loaded.)* Am I Joe? Well I've got a hunch that might be about to change. Because he's out. Terry's loose in Govanhill. And he's hungry.

The door in front of them opens. It's DEMI. She has the baby on her shoulder. No one speaks for a wee while…

DEMI: Yes?

JOE ONE: Em… Okay. Sorry. *(Still reeling from the fight with JOE and without thinking…)* Excuse me Mam, we are not Mormons. We are currently in Glasgow on a mission from our church to spread the word of Jesus Christ our Lord and saviour and to ask if you have ever felt that something is missing in your spiritual life, and if so, would you like to talk to us about what the Christian way can offer someone in your current situation? We're not Mormons.

DEMI: Yes.

Beat.

JOE ONE: Pardon me Mam?

DEMI: You got lucky. I *would,* very much, like to talk about all of the above.

The two JOES look at each other, bewildered. Big pause.

DEMI: What's the problem?

JOE ONE: Oh no problem, it's just that…well…no one has ever invited us in before. You'll be our first.

DEMI: Don't worry. I'll be gentle.

She turns and disappears into the flat. The two JOES shrug and then follow her in.

The police helicopter buzzes overhead.

PETER and JULIA in her studio. Following on.

PETER's soundscape is playing on tinny laptop speakers and he nods along to the beat. JULIA is sitting on the floor crying.

PETER: It's actually got a wee hint of gospel in there. Hear it? *(Sings a little of the melody.)* I gonna work on this section. Too bloody...coy. Know what I mean? Beef up the bottom end a bit. *(Answering a question that was never asked.)* Aye, I used to be in bands an' that, but it's a sinking ship. Ever heard of Individual Errors? That was me. Brace Yourself Rodney? Judgemental Chemist? That was more of a side project. The Chocolate Shiltons? My Tempting Sister? Learningcurve? That was me too. Well, it was a collective but I was running it. The music business is a sinking ship, man. I nearly drowned. Sounds mental saying it like that, but I did. Everyone else seemed to have a plan B and swam to shore, got jobs and lives and that, but not me. I went under. I'm only just coming up, Julia. But sometimes I think something happened when I was down there. Know what I mean? Like water got in and stuff. And now I just...don't work right. I'm only half alive. Know what I mean?

JULIA: *(Screaming.)* YES! Yes, I know what you mean! I know what it means to be half alive! That's the fucking problem here! Remember?

PETER: Oh, right. Aye. So it is. Sorry, I'm... I find it hard to get my head round things. Temperature. Look, don't cry. You're not invisible. I can see you as clear as day. Mind you... *(An idea.)* Oh! Right. Second opinion. What if we find a policeman. There's loads knocking about. If a policeman looked you in the eye and said, 'you have not disappeared – you are not the girl we're looking for', do you think that might sort things out? You could do the show?

A beat or two before JULIA decides.

JULIA: Okay.

PETER: Sorted.

JULIA: It can't be me though. Lulu should go.

JULIA gets up.

PETER: Who's Lulu?

JULIA starts to get changed into the Lulu dress and wig. PETER watches her undress – hypnotised by her body. After a moment...

PETER: God, it would be nice though, so it would...to thingme...to have a life like yours, that's got nothing to do with reality or whatever. See when you have a baby all you can think about is real life. You're trapped in it. It's like being ill. I'm ill. They don't know what it is. Virus or something. I just can't shake it. Since wee Al was born I've had 'ailments'. I didn't have ailments before I don't think. Infections and strains. Bugs and skin things and that. Colds just linger on forever. I can't remember what it's like to be well. I'm burning up, Julia.

JULIA is now dressed as 'Lulu'.

JULIA: My name is Lulu.

Beat.

PETER: See after this, Lulu...we should totally start a band.

RAJ and KULDEV in the park following on...

KULDEV: Let's do it.

RAJ: Yeah?

KULDEV: Yeah.

RAJ: The Voice of Youth. Welcome to the future.

They shake hands.

KULDEV: So, em...what happens now?

RAJ: I'll be your mentor. Which is great. I'll be an awesome mentor.

KULDEV: Yeah but…like, what can I do? Now.

RAJ: Now? Leaflets. Then tomorrow the speech.

KULDEV: But I was doing that already. That was my Property Management work experience. I want Oligarch work experience.

RAJ: Well sometimes they overlap. It'll all become clear when we sit down and go through it bit by bit. Maybe I'll do some kind of presentation with colour coding and stuff?

KULDEV: No. Look, I'm ready right now. I want to instigate. Today.

RAJ: Well you can't.

KULDEV: Oh yes I fucking can.

RAJ: But…

KULDEV: Maybe I'll go to that flat in Albert Avenue? The one you really want. And maybe I'll persuade that woman that the time has come to sell up and move on? How about that? Big time instigation.

RAJ: You don't know what to do though.

KULDEV changes. He's suddenly very threatening…

KULDEV: 'You are in danger here…living here is no life…for you… I am the Voice of Youth.'

He holds RAJ's eye for a beat then fakes a lunge at him. RAJ instinctively pulls back. After he regains composure…laughing that off, nervously…

RAJ: Ha. You're full of surprises aren't you, Twinkle? *(Pause.)* Okay doaky. Time for some quick-fire mentoring. Follow me.

KULDEV: Where we going?

RAJ: Inex Homecare. We're gonna get you a balaclava.

RAJ and KULDEV exit.

# #

JULIA and PETER arrive at the gates of Queens Park. JULIA is frantic, freaking out. She has a bag with her. PETER lags behind a bit, feeling very, very ill.

JULIA: There's no one here!

PETER: Maybe they're em…

JULIA: There's literally no one here. Look. No one. Oh god.

PETER: It is quiet. Someone'll be by in a minute. Bound to be. Let's just wait.

JULIA: No. This is…something's wrong. *(Beginning to panic.)* And look…no one in Victoria Rd. Have you ever seen that before? Literally no one! It's a desert.

PETER: God, I don't feel well at all. Going to boak I think. Stand back. I'm supposed to be opening the shop, but…oh god.

JULIA's panic steps up a notch.

JULIA: This is it. I've crossed over. Maybe that's how it happens? Maybe death is just a slow fade towards the invisible? Everything…just…vanishes, bit by bit. Shit. I'm a ghost!

PETER: Naw, it's not death it's just…mental. Christ, I feel… Christ.

PETER collapses. JULIA turns but doesn't go to him.

PETER: *(From the ground.)* Julia. Gonnie phone Demi? Tell her…

JULIA: I'm Lulu. And I don't exist. I can't be heard anymore. I cannot speak. I'm unloved and unliving. So I don't think I can be of any help really.

PETER: *(Struggling.)* Eh? Fuck sake. I just need… I need an adult. Where are the fucking adults? Christ, I feel … *(A new voice and pointing an accusing finger at JULIA.)* Ye wives… be in subjection to your own husbands! Let it not be that outward adorning of plaiting the hair, and of wearing of gold, or of putting on of apparel…

JULIA: *(Scared.)* What?

PETER: But let it be the hidden man of the heart, in that which is not corruptible. So it is.

JULIA: What's wrong with you? Why are you speaking like that?

PETER: The world of Man awaits before the Gates with hands of blood. You are the chosen victim of his judging act. Do not fear he who destroys so seeds may grow! For it is better, if the will of God be so, that ye suffer for well doing, than for evil doing. Know what I mean? Fucking. So it is.

JULIA is stricken. She looks around. There's still no one in sight. She's terrified. Alone. Where will she go? She looks into the park. She nods. Yup. That's where I belong.

She throws her bag down and runs through the gate.

PETER: No!

The gates slam shut behind her with a huge crash.

PETER collapses again. Unconscious.

In PETER and DEMI's flat.

There is a washing basket on the floor, piled with clothes. An ironing board is set up – the iron is unplugged and has the cord wrapped around the base. DEMI is struggling with the baby. He's screaming the place down. She paces back and forward, bounces up and down, anything to calm him down. Nothing works...

DEMI: Oh please...please...shoosh shoosh shoosh...please... what is it? What's *wrong*? I... I... I don't know what else to do darling...there's nothing else to try. Please... Mummy needs to... Mummy needs to live...what is it? I don't know what to do.

She has an idea. It's a long shot. She gets down on her knees. The baby goes slightly quieter...

DEMI: *(A prayer.)* Dear God...

The doorbell rings. Baby Al is suddenly quiet.

DEMI can't believe it. Almost laughs…

DEMI: *(To God.)* Please hold. Your calling is very important to me.

She opens the door to reveal JOE ONE…on his own.

This is the end of the previous JOES and DEMI scene, but from DEMI's point of view.

To repeat…there is no JOE TWO.

No one speaks for a wee while…

DEMI: Yes?

JOE ONE: Em…Okay. Sorry. *(Still reeling from the fight with JOE and without thinking…)* Excuse me Mam, we are not Mormons. We are currently in Glasgow on a mission from our church to spread the word of Jesus Christ our Lord and saviour and to ask if you have ever felt that something is missing in your spiritual life, and if so, would you like to talk to us about what the Christian way can offer someone in your current situation? We're not Mormons.

DEMI: Yes.

Beat.

JOE ONE: Pardon me Mam?

DEMI: You got lucky. I *would,* very much, like to talk about all of the above.

JOE looks to his right. Big pause.

DEMI: What's the problem?

JOE ONE: Oh no problem, it's just that…well…no one has ever invited us in before. You'll be our first.

DEMI: Don't worry. I'll be gentle.

She waves him into the flat. He looks terrified.

DEMI: He's just this second dropped off and I'm going to attempt to stretch it into a nap. Won't work but it's worth a shot. I'm supposed to be somewhere else actually, but he had other plans. As usual. I was once renowned for being bang on time, but now things are…more flexible, shall we say. Sometimes I just don't show up to stuff. No one seems to notice. Would you like a drink or something?

JOE ONE: *(To invisible JOE TWO.)* I wasn't going to, Joe. No I wasn't. Em. I *am* controlling it. Okay.

DEMI: Pardon?

JOE ONE: Perhaps if I had a glass of water, Mam? Lower your voice. Joe. Lower your voice. I'm sorry. Nerves.

DEMI: Uh huh. Two ticks.

DEMI goes off to get a glass of water and put Al in his cot. She's getting an uneasy feeling about all of this. JOE ONE sits and holds his head.

JOE ONE: I'm not !

JOE TWO is right beside him now.

JOE TWO: Then why are you holding your head? I'm worried. Look.

JOE TWO lifts some of DEMI's underwear from the washing pile.

JOE TWO: The devil can take many forms Joe. What if...

As DEMI enters, JOE TWO disappears. DEMI has put the baby down in the next room. She has a glass of water for JOE.

DEMI: I doubt he'll sleep. No one can. It's so hot.

JOE ONE looks ill. He has to summon a lot of energy to make conversation...

JOE ONE: Oh we're...used to it...

DEMI hands over the glass which JOE ONE tries to hold but can't. His hands are numb. The glass slips to the floor and smashes.

DEMI: Shit.

JOE ONE: My...my hands...

DEMI: It's all right.

Just as she goes to clear it up something massive flies overhead, pitching the scene into darkness with a huge, loud swoosh.

DEMI: There's that sound again. Christ it's getting worse.

When it passes and we can see again, both JOES are standing behind DEMI. She can't see them. She's preoccupied, looking up, out of the window, trying to find what's making that hellish noise.

JOE TWO: He's here. Terry's here!

JOE TWO runs off through the front door. Leaving JOE ONE alone with DEMI. JOE ONE looks entirely different – dangerous now.

DEMI turns. She can see that things aren't normal.

DEMI: What's wrong?

JOE ONE: I can't remember.

DEMI: Should we...do you want to say a prayer or something?

JOE ONE: *(Shakes his head.)* It doesn't work.

JOE ONE moves towards DEMI. He has his fists clenched and is breathing quickly...

There's a knock at the door. JOE stops. DEMI and JOE watch the door slowly open.

It's KULDEV. He's ditched the blazer and has his face covered in a balaclava.

He comes into the room. Stepping immediately into some kind of standoff. He's thinking...what...the...fuck?

Confidently, DEMI lifts up the iron and weighs it in her hand, like a weapon.

DEMI: My son is sleeping in the next room. Let's get this done.

There is a massive shriek – TERRY's war cry.

The Govanhill baths. It's empty. It's not much later than when we were here last, but there's an uncanny, eerie atmosphere now.

There's a thud from above. The whole place trembles. A massive shadow is cast over the whole scene. An instant change in atmosphere.

A distant smash from high above us.

Glass falls like snow, tinkling on the tiles musically. Then...

Slowly…

TERRY descends.

His huge wings are spread to their full span and fill the stage. His eyes glow a familiar red. He lands on the bottom of the condemned pool with a deep sigh, casting a cloud of dirt and glass around him with a whoosh.

It's hard to make him out properly in this light, but we can be damn sure that this is who JOE TWO was on about.

The police helicopter is buzzing angrily, hovering above; bringing with it a racket of street sounds. It's a nasty mix of worlds this.

The search light swoops down through the skylight. When it catches TERRY we get our only full look at him. Just a glimpse in the fast flashing light, but God it's enough. He's skeletal. His skin is parachute-thin and his movements are halting.

TERRY lets the world know that he's not done yet. He lets out an ear-splitting, territory-marking scream.

It's a whole new sound.

THREE

The next day.

The Govanhill Baths in daylight. It has been dressed and prepped for tonight's rally – banners, stacked chairs etc. JULIA's stuff has been cleared away. There is a lectern set up with a microphone.

JOE pops his head up from the darkness of the pool.

JOE TWO: They've gone. Joe, they've gone.

> *JOE ONE appears from his hiding place. His clothes are covered in dried blood. His face shows the marks of his fight with DEMI. He's frightened and pretty out of it…*

JOE ONE: For sure?

JOE TWO: I thought they'd never get done.

JOE ONE: We can't be here. We have to go, Joe. People are coming. They were setting up for some kind of event. *(Points at a banner.)* Look. That's tonight. We have to get out of here, man.

JOE TWO: We can't go back to the apartment.

JOE ONE: No.

JOE TWO: They'll be looking for you there.

JOE ONE: Maybe we could…maybe we need to run?

JOE TWO: To the States? How Joe? We have no money. You're a wanted man. We need some food, is the first thing.

> *JOE ONE staggers a bit and sits on the edge of the pool. He puts his head in his hands and cries.*

JOE TWO: Hey. Don't cry Joe. I'll get us out of here. Don't you worry, Joe. I'll find a way.

JOE ONE: I… I can't remember it. Can't remember anything.

JOE TWO: That's the concussion Joe.

JOE ONE: No Joe. No it's deeper than that. It's been weeks, man. *(Shaking his head.)* I can't remember where I come from. I can't remember my parents. My house. I've tried. But there's nothing there.

JOE TWO: That's all in the past anyway Joe…

JOE ONE: I heard Brother Kyle saying I had 'substance issues' but…

JOE TWO: You had an unsettled home life, Joe, that's all you need to know. This wasn't your fault. It's best that you don't remember. Block it out. No court in the land could blame you for what happened yesterday. That woman attacked you with an iron! She wanted to kill you! Look at your face Joe! If Terry hadn't led us here…

JOE ONE: Brother Kyle said it was my medication confusing me. So we threw it in the park. That's as far back as I can remember.

JOE TWO: Praise Jesus for that Joe. Can I get an Amen?

JOE ONE: Where do I come from, man?

JOE TWO: Let me hear an Amen!

JOE ONE: Why can't I remember?

JOE TWO: Just say Amen, Joe!

JOE ONE: What's making me do this? What is it!?

JOE TWO: *(Shouting above him.)* Amen! Just say it. Say it!

JOE ONE: Amen.

JOE TWO: Thank you. Gosh. It's just simple manners is all. Say, talking of manners…you probably don't want to hear this now Joe, but I think you owe Terry an apology. If it weren't for him you'd be done for. He turned up when the going got tough and led us to freedom. He led us here. Whether you remember it or not, that's what happened.

A beat. JOE ONE looks at JOE TWO.

JOE ONE: Where is he?

JOE TWO: Say again?

JOE ONE: Where is he Joe?

JOE TWO: *(Defensive.)* He's resting.

JOE ONE: I thought he'd vanished?

JOE TWO: He returned. Thanks be to Jesus. You saw him!

JOE ONE: I saw nothing man.

JOE TWO: Well… I don't know what to tell you Joe. He came back. We followed. He saved the day, whether you believe in him or not.

Beat.

JOE ONE: Go get him then Joe.

Big pause. A standoff.

JOE TWO: *(Shrugs.)* Whatever you say Joe.

JOE TWO jumps down into the darkness of the pool.

A hospital room in the New Victoria Infirmary. PETER lies, unconscious, in a hospital bed.

Baby Al is asleep in his buggy. DEMI is pacing up and down. Adrenalin still pounds through her veins. She's reliving her battle with JOE and KULDEV, blow by blow – not for the first time – and she is loving it!

DEMI: I knew I'd win. The fact that Al was in the next room made it seem like a foregone conclusion. You cannot get past me! I will fight to the death! And I did. Well, not to the death but you know what I mean. I went for the little American guy first. BOOSH! A hard sweep from me and down he goes. The guy in the balaclava turned to run and I was like that 'no way!' Ran to the door, kicked it shut and threw him to the floor. I had super strength. He was like a doll. BAM! The American ran, blood streaming from his face. Out into the close and away. Then the balaclava boy tries to run too, but I'm on him. Pounding him. Punch, punch, punching him. I pull the balaclava off and it's stuck to his face with all the blood. There's wool in his wound. And it's a kid! Just some Asian kid. I hold his throat with one hand and call the cops with the other. It took them… I dunno…ten minutes to get there…but that whole time I just held his throat. We never spoke. Not one word. He just seemed to get younger and younger, under my hand. And I'm just smiling at him. Happier than I've been in… I dunno.

I was attacked. I fended. I fought. I defended my child… with violence! Jesus…it feels so… I did what I was supposed to do. Know what I mean? And Al went straight down! It was a miracle. In a quiet flat he screams the place down, but when Mummy's next door battering two assailants he's spark out. I don't remember reading about that particular wind-down technique in my Gina Ford book. Mind you I threw my Gina Ford book in the swan pond so… God.

Everything's great now.

Pause.

DEMI checks to see if there's any change in PETER. No. She looks out the window. Filling the silence…

DEMI: I remember when this hospital wasn't here. Just an old, derelict school. Doesn't seem that long ago. And then – poof! – it appeared. I never thought I'd live here long enough to see changes like that. But in a city that stuff is…constant. Isn't it? The skyline's just spinning plates. I wonder if I'll die in one of these rooms? Or in a hospital that's yet to be built?

I fought. I won. We win. We forget that good guys can win. Young people know it, but we've forgotten.

You're so scared of young people. I don't know why. Maybe you get it from the papers or something? Every page. Every day. Kids attacking people, kids being attacked…it's like we're at war with children. And for what? Youth? Is that the prize? Christ. It wasn't that good. I'm sorry Peter but it wasn't. And yet you still dress like them, you act like them…trainers and T-shirts, action figures and all the latest phones and gizmos. You read magazines about computer games for Christ sake! You need to choose a side, Peter. You really do.

Another pause. She's at a bit of a loss.

DEMI: Em. Well. They said to keep talking so…em… I'm just going to tell you it all again, okay? It's inspirational. Al was kicking off and I'd tried everything to get him down with no joy. I was at my wit's end when suddenly the doorbell goes and he is…miraculously… silent.

# #

In RAJ's office in Allison Street. It's a property management business on a very small scale. One desk, a couple of plastic chairs, some files on the floor. There are the details of some flats on the wall, but not many.

RAJ has just stood up from behind his desk. KULDEV has just walked in through the door. RAJ is trying very hard to keep this jovial and re-establish yesterday's pecking order. KULDEV has his coat on and has come straight from the jail. He is having none of this. He's hard. His face is bruised. He has made some big decisions.

RAJ: Heeeeeeyyyyyy!!!!! Here he is. The Birdman of Alcatraz! Live from Folsom Prison! Straight out of chokey! Norman… Stanley…

KULDEV: I want my blazer back.

RAJ: I got you a present.

RAJ hands KULDEV a box file. KULDEV opens it and pulls out a Greggs bag. There's a cupcake inside.

RAJ: It's a file with a cake in it. It's a gag. Normally people give prisoners a cake with a file in it, but I've…oh lighten up Twinkle for fuck sake!

KULDEV: I'm not a prisoner. And my name is not Twinkle.

Beat.

RAJ: No charges?

KULDEV: They can't hold me. My cousin is a human rights lawyer. He put on quite a show. I'm a schoolboy covered in blood. It all depends what the woman does next.

RAJ: What did you say you were doing there?

KULDEV: I want my blazer back.

RAJ gets KULDEV his blazer.

RAJ: Listen… I'll handle her. She's all talk. I'll have a word in her ear and it'll all vanish. Trust me. And okay, you spent the night in jail and took a few blows, but actually…big picture…this worked a treat. What's the bet that they were on the phone to their estate agent first thing this morning?

KULDEV: Have you ever been hit like that?

RAJ: Oligarchs come from the streets, man. What do you think?

KULDEV: I don't think you've ever been hit like that. And I don't think you've ever spent the night in jail either.

RAJ: I've been careful.

KULDEV: You're not an Oligarch.

RAJ: Not yet.

KULDEV: Not ever. You've been playing. For all the dodgy scams, you're still just playing.

RAJ: Be careful you.

KULDEV: Yeah. I should be careful. Especially when it comes to my choice of mentor. I don't think I want to be sold again.

RAJ: Oh, so I 'sold' you did I? Oh boo hoo. It was your idea! Remember? You talked me into it! I've never threatened someone face to face. Not ever. I should've stuck to my guns. I'm exposed now!

KULDEV: *(Overlapping.)* I was sitting in there thinking…to get what I want…to be a Big Dog…real power…real money… then I cannot be sold for someone else's profit. Never again.

Beat.

RAJ: So what did you tell them? About me? Did you grass me in, you little shit? Bet you did. Are they coming?

KULDEV puts his blazer on.

KULDEV: You're a prize fighter. Let the imagination prepare the reality.

RAJ: What's that supposed to mean?

KULDEV: I'll tell you what I told the police. Check out my 'Voice of Youth' speech at the rally tonight.

RAJ: Why? What are you going to say? Oh, you going to unmask me as the great villain of the Southside ? Let the press call me Fagin and the cops lock me up? Yeah, right. It won't work. No one will believe you.

KULDEV: Maybe. Or maybe I'll just do the speech as written. 'I am in danger...'

A pause. RAJ changes tone...

RAJ: Look. Let me talk to her. I know her. I can sort this in ten minutes flat. You won't be charged, your record will remain unblemished, it's all a misunderstanding, blah blah blah. Back you go to school, your prefect badge gleaming and your family untroubled. Then we can get down to business. Me and you.

KULDEV: I'm making a move Raj. I'm stepping up. See you at the rally.

KULDEV goes.

RAJ: *(Shouting after him.)* I'll sort this!

#

The baths. The JOES. JOE TWO is down in the darkness getting TERRY.

JOE TWO: *(Off.)* I was thinking Joe. If he's up to it, maybe Terry could be persuaded to fly down to our Head Office and get us some help?

JOE ONE: And how would he do that Joe?

JOE TWO: *(Off.)* Huh?

JOE ONE: How could Terry get help Joe?

JOE TWO: *(Off.)* You know. Call the cavalry. Okay, you've left a message, but did they receive it is the question? We need a Deep Clean. Deep. The Monsters have blood on their hands now Joe.

JOE ONE: I mean how would he indicate to the Fathers at Head Office that anything was wrong?

JOE TWO: *(Off.)* He'd tell them.

JOE ONE: What?

JOE TWO: *(Appearing.)* He'd tell them.

JOE TWO appears from the darkness of the deep end. He has TERRY with him on a lead.

TERRY is immense – stunning.

He has red eyes. He stretches his wings.

JOE ONE screams. His eyes widen, his jaw drops…

JOE TWO: Terry can talk now Joe. Honestly, I'm as surprised as you. He just started talking. Not all of it makes sense of course, and he could work on his diction, but even so, I think it's pretty good for a…you know…dinosaur or whatever.

JOE ONE: Wh…what does he say?

JOE TWO: All kinds of junk. I reckon we could teach him a message for the Head Office though, no sweat. 'Angels Met Devil in Glasgow. Horrific Consequences. Deep Clean Required. Yours Sincerely Joe and Joe.'

JOE ONE: How does he…? How do you get him to…?

JOE TWO starts to tug on TERRY's lead. He gets no response. He tries a few different techniques. Nothing.

JOE TWO: I don't know. Maybe he has nothing to…

TERRY: FUCKING
WELCOME TO YOUR GORY BED
OR TO VICTORIE
AN THAT
SO IT IS
KNOW WHAT I MEAN.

JOE TWO: Okay Terry! Listen up… 'Angels met the Devil…' Terry concentrate… 'Deep clean required urgently…' Terry! Stay! Terry!

TERRY is rebelling: up on his back legs flapping his massive wings to full span. JOE TWO is pulled off his feet as TERRY slips loose his chains. JOE TWO has lost control…

TERRY: FUCKING
IN SHAPE O BEAST
A TOUZIE TYKE,
BLACK GRIM AND LARGE
SO IT IS

JOE TWO: No Terry! Bad! Tell them: 'Glasgow Mission in danger… Angel bludgeoned…'

TERRY: AND FIDGIN FAIN
AND HOTCH'D AND BLEW WI MIGHT AND MAIN
FUCKING
HINGME
DEEP CLEAN!
DEEP CLEAN!

TERRY flaps his wings and takes off. JOE ONE is blown from his feet by the gust as TERRY soars up, off through the skylight.

JOE TWO: Terry! I didn't tell you where you're going! You don't know the address Terry! Come back! Terry!

He's gone with a swoosh and a shriek.

JOE TWO: Ah shoot! Joe we gotta go get him. Come on!

JOE TWO runs off to chase TERRY.

JOE ONE is frozen to the spot, staring. His eyes are locked on

CHRIST/SIN sign, visible through the shattered skylight.

PETER is dancing.

He's outside the gates of Queens Park, but not as we know it.

He's lit by a huge mirror ball and thousands of fairy lights which are entwined around the railings. The sky is a weird colour.

Behind the closed gates are two red eyes. It's TERRY.

Music thumps. And PETER is loving it!

PETER: I'm loving this!

TERRY: FUCKING
    IS IT THE CURE?
    MATE?
    IS THIS HINGME?
    THE CURE THAT'S ON?

PETER: No! This is me. This is my soundscape!

TERRY: NO WAY.
    SOUNDS LIKE DISINTEGRATION-ERA CURE
    SO IT DOES.

PETER stops dancing.

PETER: How does it? Shut up! Who are you anyway?

TERRY: FUCKING
    I WAS LIKE THAT
    O MAN!
    WHILE IN THY EARLY YEARS
    HOW PRODIGAL OF TIME!
    MIS-SPENDING ALL THY PRECIOUS HOURS,
    THY GLORIOUS PRIME!
    ALTERNATE FOLLIES TAKE THE SWAY;
    LICENTIOUS PASSIONS BURN
    WHICH TENFOLD FORCE GIVE NATURE'S LAW:
    THAT MAN WAS MADE TO MOURN
    SO HE WAS
    KNOW WHIT I MEAN?

No. He doesn't. But whatever, he's happy. PETER dances again.

PETER: Shit man, I am loving it here. Wooooooooo!!!!!! How come I love it here so much?

TERRY: JIST COS.
    SEE HERE
    THIS IS THE PLACE WHERE YOU DON'T NEED
    TO GIVE A SHIT.

PETER: Is it heaven?

TERRY: NEVER SAID IT WIS HEAVEN
I SAYS IT'S WHERE YOU DINNAE NEED TAE GIE
A SHIT.
CAREFREE AN THAT
KNOW WHAT I MEAN?

PETER: Yeah. Yeah! Carefree? Wow. I'm carefree. See caring about stuff? Wears me out so it does. I fucking hate it actually. I pretend to care cos I should, but God, it's graft. Know what I mean? Demi loves it. She gets angry about stuff in the papers and goes to meetings and everything. On Tuesday nights! See those cold, dark Tuesday night church hall committee meetings… Let me tell you man… the world is run by people who like going to those meetings. Which is another way of saying the world is run by… *(He's stopped dead by a thought.)* Shit. Am I mad? Is that what this is?

TERRY: FUCKING
O THOU PALE ORB
THAT SILENT SHINES
WHILE CARE-UNTROUBLED MORTALS SLEEP
THOU SEEST A WRETCH, WHO INLY PINES
AND WANDERS HERE TO WAIL AND WEEP!
WITH WOE I NIGHTLY VIGILS KEEP
BENEATH THY WAN UNWARMING BEAM
AND MOURN, IN LAMANTATION DEEP
HOW LIFE AND LOVE ARE ALL A DREAM!
KNOW WHAT I MEAN
BY THE WAY
FUCKING
SO IT IS

#

PETER lies in his hospital bed. JULIA is there, dressed as Lulu. She looks dishevelled and unslept. She stands looking into Al's buggy.

JULIA: It's actually a relief being a ghost. No one can see me, so nobody cares. And when nobody cares then you're really free. No ambition needed. No judgements. No attempt – so no failure. And I don't have any thoughts either. Which is cool. I just let the wind blow me…through the park…down the alleyways of Govanhill…when I get tired I walk through walls all the way home. But it's… unresolved, somehow. Half and half. It's not like the stories. You still get hungry.

DEMI comes in to the room with a coffee.

DEMI: Oh. Hi.

JULIA: Can…can you see me?

DEMI: *(The coffee.)* You want this? I don't think I'll touch it. Just needed something to do.

JULIA ignores the coffee…

JULIA: You can see ghosts. Did you know that? That means something. Maybe you're half alive half dead? Like me. Could it be that?

DEMI: Okay. Sorry, and you are?

JULIA: I'm Lulu.

DEMI: Demi.

JULIA: Demi! Ah. Right. Yeah. From the Rally. I would've been performing at that. Had I not passed on.

DEMI: Oh. Right. Yeah. Are you the…performance…person?

JULIA: I was, but unfortunately…

DEMI: *(Bulldozing over her.)* I take it you're here for this. *(She digs a file out from under the buggy.)* That's everything… running order, phone numbers, who's doing what at the get-out. I'll try to be down, but as you can see… I have *this. (Brightening.)* And you've probably heard that I was attacked? Yeah. In my home. Two guys. They wanted to kill me. I fought them though. With my hands and legs.

One was American – he got away. I was the winner. Their blood sprayed up.

JULIA: Attacked? And you didn't die?

DEMI: No. I won. It's inspirational. *(The file.)* If you could take that down to the Govanhill Baths it would be a great help. Okay?

JULIA: *(Taking the file.)* I might be at the baths… I might not. Sometimes I just haunt places. It's kinda hard to predict. See all this mess on my clothes? That's grave dirt.

DEMI: But that's what you're here for, right? Someone from the committee sent you? You don't need anything else? Raj Singh has the keys so I…

JULIA: *(PETER.)* I thought I was here for him. But maybe it was to meet you. I go where the wind blows me.

DEMI: You know Peter?

JULIA: I don't feel guilty for leaving him there or anything. I had no choice. I had to run. Back to the park. Where I was last seen. But I suppose, I wanted to make sure someone was looking after him in the real world. Unlike me.

DEMI: *(A little harder.)* I'm looking after him. So… You were there? At the gates?

JULIA: Yeah. He wants to live in a fantasy world with me. He wants us to start a band.

DEMI: Is that right?

JULIA: Don't worry. It's not going to happen. I vanished.

DEMI: Right. Maybe you should try vanishing again? Rematerialize down at the baths and make yourself useful.

JULIA: I go where the wind blows me.

DEMI comes over to JULIA. Something in DEMI's swagger makes JULIA back away.

DEMI blows on JULIA.

JULIA goes to the door and turns…

JULIA: *(With edge.)* Is he going to die then?

DEMI: What?

> *That thought had never occurred to DEMI. She goes to PETER and sees him lying there, as if for the first time…*

DEMI: Of course he's not going to die! Why would you say that?

JULIA: *(Softer.)* Sorry, I… I'm seeing things from the other side. You're lucky, in a way. You get to be the strong one. He lets you play that role. Doesn't he? I wonder if that'll be different when he dies? I hope not. I hope you can be strong without him beside you being weak.

DEMI: He's not going to die!

Back at the Gates. PETER and TERRY's eyes.

PETER tries to open the gates. Sparks fly, the lights flicker and he's thrown backwards in agony.

PETER: AH! Fucking hell! The gates of Heaven are electrified? Is that something people know?

TERRY: NAEBDAY SAYD IT WIS THE GATES OF HEAVEN!

PETER: Shit man. What's in there then?

TERRY: NORMAL PARK SHIT.
FAMILIES. JOGGERS. PENSIONERS. DUGS.

PETER: Missing girls?

TERRY: AYE.
THEM IN AW.

PETER: Is she in there? The girl that didn't come home?

TERRY: IF SHE ISANE, THEN THEY'LL BE A GIRL THAT LOOKS JIST LIKE HER.
IT'S FOO AY THEM.
AN MUCH WORSE IN AW.

PETER: What? Monsters?

TERRY: WHIT DAE YOU HINK?

PETER: Christ. There's just a railing between me and you. Monsters on one side, us on the other. On our side we go to work and bring up kids. On your side…missing girls… murder…horror… God knows what. And in between…a bloody railing. That's the kinda shit I cannae cope with.

TERRY: IT'S THE WAY IT'S EYWAYS BEEN
IN A CITY
KNOW WHIT I MEAN?
IT'S THE PRICE YOU PAY FOR HAVING WORK
AND EXCITEMENT AND OPPURTUNITY RIGHT
ON YOUR DOORSTEP.
THE WORLD IS HERE, KNOW WHAT I MEAN?
THE WORLD IS GOOD
AND THE WORLD IS BAD.
YE CANNAE HIDE FAE THAT SHIT IN A CITY.
YE CANNAE HIDE AT AW.

PETER: I cannae cope with that though. I just…the fear of what could happen kinda freezes me. Keeps me awake at night. Hey, wait a minute. I thought you said this was where I didn't need to care?

TERRY: IT IS.

PETER: So how come I'm thinking about all this stuff now?

TERRY: DUNNO.
MAYBE IT'S JIST THE WAY YE UR?
MAYBE YER A TUESDAY NIGHT MEETING
PERSON AFTERALL?
A NATURAL CARER.
THE WORLD IS RUN BY FOLK LIKE YOU
MAYBE YOU'RE A CITY BOY AT HEART?
KNOW WHAT I MEAN?
YOU WANT YER KID TO HAVE ALL THE COOL
STUFF THAT A CITY BRINGS
AN THAT MEANS DEALING WITH THE SHIT ON
THE OTHER SIDE OF THIS RAILING.

OR SOMETHING.

FUCK IT MAN, I DON'T KNOW.

WILL I JIST STICK THE TUNES BACK ON?

PETER: *(Angry.)* Aye! Stick the tunes on! Sake.

The music comes back on. PETER tries to dance, but can't keep it up.

PETER: Ach. It sounds shit now.

PETER stirs in his hospital bed. DEMI strokes his forehead. She's worried. She looks up. Can she hear the music? Where's it coming from?

The hospital scene and the scene at the gates are beginning to bleed into each other slightly...

RAJ appears in the door. He has a large bunch of flowers with him and a bag of sweets. DEMI can't stand RAJ.

RAJ: Mrs. Stone. My God, eh?

DEMI: Oh. Right. Mr Singh. Em...

RAJ: Oh, Raj, please. And it was no trouble. Of course I came as soon as I heard. I have tablet.

DEMI: Yeah. Em. Can you hear music or..?

RAJ: *(Shakes his head.)* And you mustn't worry. The rally. It's handled. I'm handling it all. That committee is a well-oiled machine, thanks to you. It'll be fine. You need to be here. And obviously the event has a slightly...*different* tone now, but it'll still work, I'm sure. Please, don't give it another thought.

DEMI: A different tone? Why? Because of what happened to me? No. That was good! I showed the Southside that if you fight back you win. That's the message we need to get out there!

RAJ: No, I mean the girl. You haven't heard? You need to get on Twitter. Izzy Whatsirname. Turns out she wasn't missing at all. She was bunked up with some guy in a caravan in Ayrshire. Came waltzing home completely unaware of the fuss she'd caused. Ha! Unbelievable. So...the police are gone and the Southside breathes again. You look disappointed.

DEMI: No. No, I'm...

RAJ: Were you hoping that perhaps the child you attacked may have been responsible for her disappearance? No. Sorry.

DEMI: *(That hits a nerve.)* No. I just... I was...

RAJ: And don't worry about him either. The boy. I've handled it.

DEMI: Handled what?

RAJ: Your victim. The boy in your flat. I've handled it. It's being dealt with, in house, so to speak. Please, put your mind to rest. Focus your energies on your husband's recovery.

DEMI: The boy in the balaclava? You know him?

RAJ: He's from a very good family. Very good. So I just want to reassure you...this will all...go away.

DEMI: Yes. Mr Singh...

RAJ: Raj.

DEMI: What are you doing here?

RAJ: Visiting. And offering assistance. I mean...You invite a young lad into your home and then attack him – that could get extremely messy in the long run. But...luckily... I know the boy. I know his father. I can smooth it all away. Easy. All you have to do is say to the police that this was all a big misunderstanding and that as far as you're concerned it's all forgotten...and we can get this put to bed and focus on the important things. Thank God, eh? It's not as bad as you think it is.

Beat.

DEMI: You know the guy?

RAJ: It's a small world.

DEMI: Isn't it? Like when you said you owned all the other flats in our close.

RAJ: Yes.

DEMI: And when I complained about the noise and smell and the people coming and going at all hours you made us a low ball offer. You would be happy to take it off our hands you said. You kept going on and on about it. Every time we meet. I wondered…why does this guy want our flat so much? And what would he do to get it?

RAJ: I'm a property manager, Mrs. Stone. That stuff… It's an instinct.

DEMI: We'll sell. Now. To you. For two hundred thousand.

RAJ: *(Laughs.)* Well. It's not worth anything like that I'm afraid. Not by a long shot. Especially now, what with the…

DEMI: *(Hard. With weight…)* You know the guy? The boy who came into my house wearing a balaclava? Am I getting that right? If the police asked, you'd say, 'Yes. I know him'.

A beat. RAJ gets it.

RAJ: Two hundred will make things very difficult for me.

DEMI: Except that this will all go away.

RAJ: You'll drop it? Completely.

DEMI: Two hundred grand… I drop it…and the flat is yours. Time for everyone to move on.

RAJ looks weak. He nods.

DEMI reaches over and takes some tablet from the poke in RAJ's hand.

DEMI: Sold.

JOE ONE is in Govanhill Baths, where we left him. Reeling.

JULIA comes in. JOE spins round, caught. But JULIA doesn't see him at first. She chucks the file that DEMI gave her down somewhere and goes to find her flight case from before – tidied away somewhere – and she absently looks through it. It's as if this stuff comes from another life.

JOE should hide, but he can't take his eyes off of JULIA. When she sees JOE she gets a fright – springs back.

Eventually…

JOE ONE: You…em…you shouldn't be here.

JULIA: I know.

JOE ONE: You should run away.

JULIA: Why?

JOE ONE: I kill people.

JULIA: What?

JOE ONE: I'm a boy who kills people.

    Big silence.

JULIE: The…the American boy?

JOE ONE: Yeah. I'm insane as well, I think. I've got dinosaurs on the brain and blood on my hands, man. You'd better just…run.

    Beat.

JULIA: But…you…em… it's me.

JOE ONE: Huh?

JULIA: It's me you're looking for.

JOE ONE: I'm not looking for…

JULIA: Yeah. You are. Or… I dunno… I'm looking for you. Shit. Jesus. Oh God. So. At last! *(Trying to be breezy but terrified and freaking out.)* Pleased to meet you, Mr Killer Man.

    JULIA breaks. She cries. Covers her face. She's hyperventilating. JOE goes to her…

JOE ONE: Hey. Are you… I… I don't think… I…are you okay?

JULIA: *(A sudden rush of determination.)* Is there anyone else here? Quick! Is there anyone else…?

JOE ONE: No. I'm hiding. People are coming though.

JULIA: Yeah. Yeah. People are coming. Okay. Then…then… okay…we should hurry then. Let's get this done.

JOE ONE: Get what done? Who are you?

JULIA: Let's just do it! Come on! Shit!

JOE ONE: Do what?

JULIA: Let's just fucking do it!

JOE ONE: Do what? I don't know what's...

JULIA: *(On the edge of hysteria.)* Kill me! Vanish me. Forever this time, no half measures. Do it! Come on! Do it, do it, do it!

Beat.

JOE ONE: Is this real though?

JULIA: Yeah.

JOE ONE: Like. Are you real? Are you alive?

Beat. Tricky question.

JULIA: I...it's...look, just do it okay? Don't think about it. We can't think about it. People are coming.

JOE ONE: But...

JULIA: Fuck sake! You've done it before. Do it again!

JULIA grabs his hands and puts them to her throat.

They stand like that for a long time. JULIA is trembling.

JULIA: I'm not having second thoughts.

JOE ONE: Okay.

JULIA: I'm not!

Another big silence.

JULIA: Is this wrong? Am I doing something wrong?

JOE ONE: I don't quite... I... I can't remember.

JULIA: Neither can I.

JOE ONE: I don't think I want to hurt you.

JULIA: Look. It's out of our hands. This is fate or something.

JOE ONE: But I...

JULIA: Come on!

JOE ONE: Yeah, I just don't think that…

JULIA: Oh fuck sake! Just start the process of the piece!

JOE ONE: I… I don't know…

JULIA: Make me disappear! You botched your first attempt and now I'm…only…half done. Finish me!

JOE ONE: But… I don't remember a first attempt. I don't remember anything.

Beat. JULIA gives up. She steps away. JOE ONE gasps for air, as he was the one being throttled and is now released…

JULIA: Okay, okay. Stop. Try to…try to visualise the communion of the piece. Yeah? Then actualise that impulse with movement. It's actually quite straightforward. Tell me how it feels when you kill and we'll impro from there.

JOE ONE: I don't know. It's just that…well…see… I know that sometimes, my hands go numb, and my head aches, and I blackout. But there's no memory. All I can remember is, just before I go blank, there's a…a feeling…a need to… kinda, kinda, bite down. Would you mind maybe we lay on the floor?

JULIA: Will it help the image?

JOE ONE: I think…yeah, maybe.

They awkwardly get down on the floor, JOE kneeing above JULIA. After a long pause…

JULIA: So, you bite us? Like a vampire or…?

JOE ONE: No. No, I *feel* like biting; not people…something. Like a baby teething, you know? I want to chow, gnaw down, until the sharpness underneath me pierces up through the gum and I can get some…release. But, like I say…blackout.

JULIA: Mm. I know that teething feeling.

JOE ONE: Yeah?

JULIA: Yeah. It comes when I'm just about to start work. But they never push through. I have a mouth full of baby teeth.

JOE ONE: Sorry, I'm Joe by the way.

JULIA: I'm Lulu.

JOE ONE: Hi Lulu.

JULIA: Actually my name is Julia.

JOE ONE: Oh. Hi Julia.

JULIA: Hi.

JOE ONE: What do you do, Julia?

JULIA: I'm an artist. I used to be. That's dead now. You killed it.

JOE ONE: Oh. Did I? Gee. I'm sorry.

JULIA: I don't mind really. I was asking for it. Do you think you can't remember what happens next, because I'm already dead? Am I short-circuiting the natural order? Because, believe me, that would be typical.

JOE ONE: No, Julia. No, it's all me. For weeks now… I just can't remember, like, anything. How I got here, where I came from…it's like a dream. They gave me medication. Which helped a little, I guess, until, you know, I threw it into the park.

JULIA: Why did you throw it in the park?

JOE ONE: I was told to. By the guy looking after me.

JULIA: Sometimes I think that the guys who are supposed to be looking after us aren't very good at looking after us. Do you ever think that?

JOE ONE: Yeah. I do think that. I just want to remember.

The pretence of a killing is long forgotten. Somewhere along the line they've held hands.

After a moment JOE ONE starts to cry. After a moment or two, JULIA starts to cry too. They look at each other. A big silence. A connection.

JULIA: Hey. It's a long shot… but there is something we could try.

# #

At the gates. PETER and TERRY. TERRY is still in the shadows. PETER is looking through JULIA's bag…

PETER: It's funny that her bag's here.

TERRY: FUCK'S FUNNY BOOT THAT?

PETER: Well. It's more odd than funny. Incongruous. Hey.

PETER pulls out the fake knife from earlier. He plays with it a bit. He finds the button that shoots fake blood.

PETER: Oh. Ha ha ha!!! It's fake. Plastic. Check it out. It shoots out stuff that looks like blood. Look. Cool.

TERRY moves forward. We can see him clearly now. PETER drops the knife in shock. He's frozen.

TERRY: PISSER
SURE IT IS
STUCK HERE WI SOMEONE LIKE ME
AND THE ONLY WEAPON TO HAND
IS A TOY.
NAE LUCK, EH?

PETER: Oh. You're the Devil.

Through the gates, PETER can see DEMI standing by his bed in the hospital.

DEMI: Peter. Please. Come on. Fight. I need you to fight. I need you.

PETER: She needs me? *(Smiling.)* No way. Hey. I can hear her. I can hear you!

DEMI: I have great news. We're getting out. We're selling up. I've got an amazing price. We can move to the country. We can get a little cottage in the middle of nowhere. Somewhere by the sea. Or in the mountains. It'll be your reward. We can hide away. I need you. I love you.

AL starts to cry…

PETER: I can hear him crying too. *(Shouting to DEMI, but she can't hear him.)* Demi! Wee Al's crying!

TERRY: AYE

YOU KIN AYEWAYS HEAR THEM CRYING.

JIST IGNORE IT.

PETER: But…he's right there…crying. And she doesn't want that. To move. Why's she saying that? And how come I'm getting a reward? I haven't done anything worth rewarding. I was gonna. I really was. I just haven't got round to it yet. *(Shouting to DEMI.)* I love you!

TERRY: YOU DON'T <u>NEED</u> TO DO ANYTHING WORTH REWARDING.

YOU DON'T NEED TO DO ANYTHING AT ALL.

PETER: I do!

TERRY: YOU DON'T

PETER: I want to!

TERRY: AYE WELL.

THAT'S AN ENTIRELY DIFFERENT FUCKING KETTLE OF FISH.

YOU WANT TO DO GOOD THINGS FOR HER?

FOR THE WEE MAN?

PETER: Yeah. Yeah.

TERRY: SOMETHING THAT WINS THEIR ADMIRATION?

WINS YOU A REWARD?

PETER: Yes!

TERRY: YOU DON'T WANT TO HIDE AWAY?

YOU DON'T WANT TO BE SCARED ANYMORE?

YOU WANT A CITY NOW?

IS THAT IT?

IS IT A FUCKING CITY YOU WANT?

PETER: I just want to get to my wife and my son. Let me get past please.

TERRY: DO YOU LOVE THESE PEOPLE ENOUGH?

PETER: Let me get past.

TERRY: ARE YOU A GOOD FATHER?
DO YOU CARE?
WILL YOU FIGHT?

DEMI: Come on Peter, fight. Fight for me.

PETER picks up the knife.

TERRY: FUCKING YAS!
HINGME
NOW'S THE DAY AND NOW'S THE HOUR
SEE THE FRONT O BATTLE LOUR
C'MON MAN.
WHIT YE SCARED OF?

PETER: *(Realising.)* Nothing.

PETER goes to the gates. Locked and electrified. He remembers something. The shop keys. He takes them out of his pocket and unlocks the chains. The gates swing open.

TERRY rises up and spreads his wings to their full span.

DEMI: Peter…you're a fighter.

PETER moves towards TERRY…

KULDEV is striding down Victoria Rd. He's back in his blazer. Just as he passes under the CHRIST/SIN sign RAJ catches up with him. RAJ is a little out of breath but bursting with Oligarch braggadocio…

RAJ: Hey! I was shouting you.

KULDEV: I didn't hear.

RAJ: Better not've been blanking me boy.

KULDEV: I didn't hear.

RAJ: Well you can sleep easy Twinkle, the big dog has sorted it.

KULDEV: Which means what?

RAJ: The woman from Albert Avenue. She's gonna go down to the police station and say she made a mistake or something. I don't know the legal details. I don't need to know and neither do you. The fact is this: you won't go to court and you won't have a record. And you've me to thank for it. I gave the bitch the full beams and she wilted in the heat. Don't like to do that so close to home, but I did. For you. So we're done. We can go back to Plan A: you stutter out the 'Voice of Youth' speech I wrote for you and tomorrow we begin Oligarch training proper. Blank page.

KULDEV: *(Unfazed.)* No. We're not doing that.

Beat.

RAJ: So…what are we doing? Are you going to stand in front of that microphone and grass me in to Glasgow as an Oligarch? Like a little fucking coward? There's no need, Kuldev. I've told you, it's finished. It's fixed. We're cool.

KULDEV: I'm not going to 'grass you in to Glasgow as an Oligarch', Raj. Know why? Cos you're *not* an Oligarch. You're *playing* at being an Oligarch. You're as much a child as everyone else.

RAJ: Bullshit. What I'm doing…

KULDEV: Is a game!

RAJ: People in this town don't aspire beyond the end of their road. That's why they're all dead by sixty-three. At least I have ambition.

KULDEV: Oh I like your ambition. But the time has come to do something real with it. Which means it's time to grow up! You want to know what I'm doing, Raj? I'm being the adult. And you can play your little games and knock things down…but adults build. So, be a good boy…stand to the side…and watch me build.

Beat. RAJ steps out of the way and KULDEV moves off.

RAJ: What are you going to say? Kuldev! What are you going to say?!

RAJ follows him off.

# #

JULIA and JOE ONE are in Govanhill Baths, where we left them.

JULIA's dance song is playing on her phone. Louder than before, filling the pool.

They are dancing. This is JULIA's show, we recognise some of the movement... JOE ONE is being led, moved, shaped and held...he's spellbound.

JOE ONE: What's supposed to happen?

JULIA: We're supposed to remember.

JOE ONE: Remember what?

JULIA: Where we come from.

JOE ONE: I don't think it's working.

JULIA: I know. That's because it doesn't work.

> *They keep dancing though. There are moments here when they are very close, skin on skin. JOE feels like he may faint. JULIA too actually.*
>
> *Then...something happens between them. JOE ONE seems to come to life. He dances <u>with</u> her, not just beside her now...he moves her... he changes...*

JOE ONE: Wait...wait a minute... I ... I remember...something...

JULIA: What, really?

JOE ONE: Keep moving. Hold me. Yeah. Yes. We danced. Just like this.

JULIA: Tell me how you danced.

JOE ONE: Like it was a secret. No. Like we didn't want to get caught.

JULIA: Like this?

JOE ONE: Like this.

JULIA: Now remember where you were.

JOE ONE: An airport.

JULIA: Now remember who else was there.

JOE ONE: A crowd of kids. Strangers. Guides. People from the organisation. Fathers, holding signs and shouting orders. There was no music. We were just holding each other.

JULIA: Now remember what you said.

JOE ONE: I said 'I don't want to go'.

JULIA: And she said 'You don't have to go'.

JOE ONE: Yeah. But I did. I had to go. I had to save her. This was my last chance.

JULIA: Was she one of your victims?

JOE ONE: No. She was my mom.

A pause.

Then JOE ONE gasps. He stumbles away from JULIA's arms. He can remember everything now. JULIA stops the music.

JOE ONE: What happened? What happened?! How did you do that?

JULIA: I don't know.

JOE ONE: I can remember now!

JULIA: I know.

JOE ONE: It was like…it was like you were inside my memory. You were inside, part of it.

JULIA: *(Amazed.)* I know! Shit! It's never worked before. Not even close.

JOE ONE: Now I know. I remember! I didn't kill anyone. I scared some people…fistfights gone too far…but all I wanted was… I dunno…to be hurt. But I didn't kill anyone, Julia. Not a single person. Not then or yesterday or… Gosh. That's a…wow, that's a relief.

JULIA: *(Getting excited.)* But it worked? Didn't it? The dance provoked a memory which in turn led to communion? Those are your exact words!

JOE ONE: *(Can't stop himself now.)* I was an addict back home. And a girl died. In the house I was in. Okay? She died right beside me. She looked a little like you.

JULIA takes off her Lulu wig.

JOE ONE: Well. Okay. She didn't really look too much like you. A guy came to our place from Mom's church– he was big, like, pumped – muscles straining the seams of his sports coat. Mom and I sat on the couch. He crouched in front of us, like a Defensive Lineman waiting for the snap. He gave me a Bible and a gun…that's the deal he said. Take your pick. It's one or the other son. He said they had a phase-out program. Get me off the meds and into God's hands. When Mom was in the kitchen he slapped my face, grabbed me by the hair. Said he didn't give a fuck about me. Said it was my mother's life he wanted to save. Not mine. But Jesus was telling him to give me another chance. His brother's name was Joe, see. And back in the 90s, this other Joe had been my age and in worse shape than me. But this other Joe had turned it all around. He saved his own life and the life of his mother through the love of Jesus Christ and hard work. If I kept this other Joe as an example, in my head, then maybe I could save my mother's life too. The Joe I'd been up to that point, he said, was extinct.

A beat or two…

JULIA: Word for word.

JOE ONE: Huh?

JULIA: You're going to say all of that again, word for word, tonight. This is…this is it! This is real. This is the…the tooth is through the gum!

JOE ONE: Tonight?

JULIA: This is the show!

JOE ONE: What do you mean?

JULIA: *(Excited.)* We do all this again – tonight. And the next night, and the next night. I dunno. But it starts tonight, yeah. Right here at the rally! So…so…stay. Okay? Just stay here. I need…time for a get in and a private space. I have to get started on some papier-mâché. Don't move.

JOE ONE: *(Confused.)* Sure.

JULIA goes to exit but stops. She pulls the flyer from her pocket and shows it to JOE.

JULIA: Hey. Do you think I look like her?

JOE ONE: No.

JULIA: *(Looking again.)* No. Me neither. We're different people.

JULIA chucks the flyer and skips away happily – looking for a room somewhere in the building.

JOE ONE is thinking it through. Just as he starts to feel good about this…a show, a girl, a memory… JOE TWO climbs out from the darkness of the pool.

JOE TWO: Joe! Come quick! Terry's been slashed! Someone got him! He's bleeding bad! He's on the Christ Died For Our Sins sign and the blood is pouring onto Victoria Road! We have to go, man!

JOE ONE closes his eyes. Is there no escape?

JOE TWO: You don't have a choice Joe. This is the only way you'll ever get home. The only way!

JOE ONE opens his eyes and follows JOE TWO as he runs off.

The Govanhill baths, a little later. The rally.

KULDEV comes to the podium. We get the impression that there is a crowd. RAJ stands behind him. RAJ is scared and ready to run. JULIA is in there too, craning her neck, looking for JOE ONE.

During KULDEV's speech some camera flashes go off, maybe his face appears on a screen…

KULDEV: I am the voice of youth. I am in danger here. Living in this area is no life at all. My ending is already written.

Right? Well. Last night I sat in a jail cell. And I thought about choice. What *choice* do I have? Carry on the way I'm going? Or turn it around? It's a choice we all have – everyone in Govanhill – right now.

Some applause.

TERRY is on top of the CHRIST/SIN sign. Bleeding heavily. The blood drips down onto Victoria Rd. The two JOES appear on the roof – beside him.

We can also see DEMI in the hospital. PETER opens his eyes.

DEMI: Peter!

PETER: I…fought.

DEMI: Yeah. We both did.

PETER: I saw it. I fought it. It's not scary when you see it close up.

DEMI: I know.

JOE TWO: Terry! Who did this to you? *(To JOE ONE.)* Jeez. He's hurt bad, Joe.

TERRY: *(With difficulty.)* I CAN STILL FLY.
SO I CAN.
ONE LAST FLIGHT.

JOE TWO: Hear that Joe! He's gonna fly us home! Praise Jesus! We'll be high in the clouds in barely a moment, Joe. Glasgow will be a tiny dot beneath us. It will fade from sight and memory with each smooth beat of his giant wings. You hear him?

JOE ONE: Yeah. Yeah, I hear him.

KULDEV: Do I retreat…behind my bedroom door…or do I stand? Well I know what happens to the kid that goes into that bedroom. And you do too. He goes into his room and he closes the door. And when he opens it again he will have become a monster. He will be unrecognisable to you. How can that be you may ask? We are decent people. We are thoughtful parents. We are concerned citizens. We go to festivals. We have the latest phones. We are members of Amnesty International and deplore injustice. We volunteer in the community. That's why we're here. Right? And yet… I promise you…what you see when your own child opens that door will chill you to the bone. Unrecognisable he will be. From another age. All-conquering. And happy to gulp up your off-white life in a snap. He may be wearing the nicest school uniform money can buy, but he'll have God in his eye, and a chib in his fist, and, under his blazer… Semtex.

The CHRIST/SIN sign flickers off. Then on again.

DEMI: We're out of here Peter. We'll selling.

PETER: No!

DEMI: Ssh. Don't… I'll get a nurse.

PETER: That's…that not what I want.

DEMI: What? What do you want? Tell me and I'll get it. Tell me…

PETER blacks out again. DEMI tries to revive him. During the following RAJ tunes in…

KULDEV: Is that what happens to me? To my entire generation? Or do I stand? Do I show the world… something else?

Well, last night, in that cell, I decided. I'm putting my hand up. I'm volunteering. Take a good look at me…look at me… I am your new politician. I am your new voice. Your new representation. With the help of prominent local business leaders *(He indicates RAJ.)* I will organise, I will protest, and I will stand for election. Playtime's over. I promise my life to activism. I will show the world something else. I will show them Glasgow.

JOE TWO: Cause all I wanna do is go home, man! I want our time here to be left like old clothes on a beach. I want to be born again, over the jagged shore of New Foundland. I want to be purified by the fires of Manhattan; baptised by the roaring water of the Great Lakes. I wanna feel that clean American air on my face. Don't you want that, Joe? Don't you want to see your mother again?

The sign flickers again…

KULDEV: Stand with me and be Glasgow. Show them Glasgow. Show them what Glasgow looks like now! Stand with me and show them that Glasgow is not a football strip stretched over the beer belly of some fat, baldy, steaming goon. No Old Firm. No Papes. No Proddies. Not here, not now. Show them something else. Show them that our bloodstream is free of any Clydebuilt disease. Not obese or rickety-legged we. Not greasy-skinned or razor-cheeked us. So show them! We do not pine for the good old days. Slums and shipyards. Nippy sweetie mammys and tackity boots. That's not us. That means nothing to us. We do not stink of fag ash. Or whiskey. Or chips. So show them something else!

JOE ONE: You go.

JOE TWO: No, we both go. Terry can make it! This is the only way.

JOE ONE: This is how you go, Joe. You fly away. You vanish. And I stay.

KULDEV: So stand with me. Stare down the barrel of Victoria Road and show them…

Show them something else! Show them that these streets are – and have always been – home. To you. To me.

And home to those who need it like a body needs water:

The Immigrant… The Refugee…this is where they come.

Applause. He has the crowd…

KULDEV: This isn't news, man – this is the way it's always been. The Irish came to this area. The Jews, the Pakistanis, the Indians, the Poles and the Czechs came to this area. The Roma came to this area. They're coming here from Syria. Pilgrims to the Southside.

Searching for a home they had on the tip of their tongue.

And they found it here. Right here!

JOE TWO: But Terry can take us from this hell to a heaven in the sky! And you want to stay? It's crazy, man! Who would want a city when they can have a heaven in the sky?

The sign flickers off.

JOE ONE: Me.

PETER: *(Waking suddenly and grabbing DEMI.)* Me! I want a city.

DEMI holds PETER.

DEMI: Yeah. I want a city too.

KULDEV: I am not afraid. I am *not* afraid! Are you? So why don't we show the bastards that! Stand with me now and be Glasgow! Come on! Be Glasgow! Be Glasgow!

THE END

www.ingramcontent.com/pod-product-compliance
Ingram Content Group UK Ltd.
Pitfield, Milton Keynes, MK11 3LW, UK
UKHW031250020325
455689UK00008B/117

9 781783 194957